Reminiscing

End of Watch
February 26, 1983

La Vie en Rose

*A Memoir of True Stories Filled with Humor,
Heartbreak and Inspiration*

by Molly Hanna Glidden

I

II

Self-published 2019

Cover design by Jennifer Quinlan of Historical Editorial

Heart in Hands, illustrated by Brooke DelMonaco

Opening photo for Chapter 18 from Pixabay, with permission
Opening photo for Chapter 28 courtesy of Ken Fitzgerald
Chapter opening photos for Chapters 5, 6, & 29 from Microsoft, with permission
All other illustrations property of Hanna family

Some names and identifying details are changed for privacy.

ISBN - 9781689786201

IV

The Hanna Family

1950 – Washington DC

Grandfather "Alfie" & Grandmother "Wawa" Hanna

George & Peg Hanna

"Georgie" & "Mary" Molly

Four children—yet to be born.

VI

Dedication

This book is dedicated to the mothers and fathers who have lost a child.

The ultimate tragedy is when a parent outlives a son or daughter.

In memory of my beloved daughter, Laura DelMonaco

To those who have lost siblings before their time.

To my dear husband who brought me sunshine when things seemed hopeless. Without you, I may not have remained strong to survive my ultimate tragedy. Thank you for reading my stories after long days at work…Love you always.

To Eli and Nancy Minkoff, who supported my writing, helping me to the finish line.

To Mike Franklyn, who believed I had another book in me.

May peace and healing be found in our less than perfect world

Contents

―――――――――

"My Red Winged Visitors" article was published in **Centering Corp. Grief Digest Magazine**, *Volume 15, Issue #2.*

XI

Introduction

In Life there's a beginning and an ending—when a child is born we are elated—when a loved one dies, we are crushed!

In between, life takes us on a journey—some take roads less traveled—others take to the highways…Whatever journey we're on, we cannot predict what lies ahead.

~~~

The following chapters are true stories—in bits and pieces—of a girl named "Mary" who grapples with many trials and tribulations—eventually facing the ultimate tragedy.

The collection of short stories has exposed parts of her secret diary. With pen in hand, her life unfolds. Molly's journey begins as a little girl named 'Mary,' fighting for her right to be called "Molly." These stories unravel her true self. She takes a stand with considerable amounts of courage, overcoming obstacles.

Molly's book is written in memory of her beautiful daughter Laura. Sharing heartfelt memories through a life cut short. Laura's passing happened while writing this book. She was her Moms best supporter and critic.

Molly's identity in elementary and middle school is her birth name Mary... The Catholic school nuns insisted she be called by her Baptismal name. Her nickname Molly was always used outside of school... Molly is derived from Mary, named after her beautiful Irish grandmother, Molly Griffin Flaherty. She too preferred the nickname over her birth name...The name Molly means, "Star of the sea."

Bits and pieces of Molly's life story are being shared to help others identify parts of their own journey. This book includes her most devastating loss. She exposes the innermost parts of her existence by sharing how strength to be a survivalist often occurs through adversity. Along with hardships, Molly shares happy times cushioning the blows. Her life depended on love, support, hope and prayer.

Without exaggeration, you will find her journey often difficult and at times seemingly impossible to navigate. By writing this book, Molly hopes her stories of growing up in the 50s and 60s will give insight into the strength it took to overcome some of life's most difficult obstacles. Tragedies continued throughout her life.

After years of unwinding trauma, my writing has been a way to express my emotional journey. My stories may be repetitive and inconsistent—they need to be told—straight from the heart.

These short narratives are works of nonfiction. There's a talent for seeing past events vividly. Memories can be fickle in nature—nevertheless—remaining true to my stories, seen through rose colored glasses. The narrative and facts are my own thoughts and views and done to the best of my ability. My hope is to bring the reader alongside me finding strength and hope. We all live through love and loss.

My Memoir told in "Bits and Pieces," completes my literary journey.

For an all embracing insight into the tragedies Molly and her family endured, her first book; **'A Family Broken, Surviving Traumatic Loss, Overcoming Tragedy,"** discloses detailed, heartbreaking loss.

My "Look Back" Glasses

Chapter 1

2018

One of my favorite things to do is revel in the sweep of nostalgia. Who doesn't like going back to capture some of those marvelous memories?

Soren Kierkegaard once wrote; *"Life can only be understood backwards; but it must be lived forwards."* Certainly putting one foot in front of the other takes us forward, but it's our past we often learn from. We tend not to dwell on past mistakes because they are commonly filled with regrets. It's best keeping our fond memories alive, filling our quiet times with the happier moments of yesteryear. When we find ourselves turning the clocks back, those older recollections do tend to appear more pleasant than the actual realities, probably due to the mind constructing our past, present, and future experiences the way we want to see them. Occasionally our past comes back in bits and pieces, like a puzzle needing to be put together. Sometimes when we tell stories, we tend to embellish things while remaining convinced of the veracity of our memories. On the flip side, when we live in the present awaiting something fun and exciting, the anticipation can be far more satisfying than the actual event.

I must say, I've had the good fortune of living long enough to be called a "senior citizen," even though it continues to be met with great resistance. For example, on my sixty-second birthday, a letter came requesting I join AARP. Feeling outraged, I called the company alerting them I was not elderly and to please unsubscribe me. Worse yet, another call came days later, asking if I needed a Lifeline! After talking the guy's ear off, I added a story about my hiking trips and my training for the Boston marathon. This guy clearly regretted cold calling me. Seriously, there's nothing more annoying than blurting out unnecessary white lies!

Truth is, I'm getting closer to the next decade of life and my denial has begun to recede. I often recall that famous quote, "Do not regret growing older. It is a privilege denied to many." There has never been a truer statement. An occasional walk down memory lane allows me to revisit with lost loved ones. In a life with so much loss, I've earned that pair of "look back" glasses, allowing me to see days of yore in rose color.

So when I sit in my chair, reverting back to my youth, I think of those days of pure innocence and discovery. In my next chapters of short stories, I will take you on a journey, as I expose raw pieces of a little girl named Mary, who taught me how to grow strong through adversity. With confidence, you will see Molly emerge.

Life's turning points

When it comes time to cross the bridge into adulthood, we begin to understand the importance of life experiences as it shapes us into who we are. Our past can enlighten us, making improvements once we allow ourselves to live each day as if it were another adventure. It's all about—*time*—giving us another chance at happiness.

Certain memories can often enhance our lives, including those occasional flashbacks. Like the day I walked into a room, and for one pleasurable moment, a scent whisked by like a gentle breeze. I delved into my memory bank, only to discover there was no way back to that moment in time. Being the type who doesn't give up easily, I decided on a Google search. Just where did that elusive but familiar fragrance come from? First I narrowed in on colognes from the 1960s, which brought up several on the internet. Then it hit me, I remembered the name of the cologne worn on my first date at 16. As the page opened, there it was, allowing me to make a purchase online. Clearly the original company no longer existed. Nevertheless, I found the exact same bottle I remembered from 50 years ago. After the purchase went through, I began feeling that exciting phase of anticipation. Wow…to once again wear my favorite cologne, "*Ambush*."

Several days had passed and the waiting was over—my package arrived! After tearing into the box and unscrewing the cap, I started to rub that familiar scent behind my ears and on my wrists. With eyes closed, I slowly began inhaling the fragrance. There I was, back in 1965 with my first love. I savored every moment as the old black and white movie played out in my head. Of course it wasn't long before my eyes gently opened and reality set in. The familiar scent seemed to evaporate into thin air and the cologne wasn't quite as nice as remembered. Everything faded as quickly as the memory… Just the same, it was worth every penny I paid. The anticipation of those happy moments in time made it all worthwhile.

It's not just flashbacks that happen when recalling old memories. Certain remembrances can bring with them a cinematic quality. These recollections can include not only happy memories but also those tragic events that remain forever vivid in the heart, soul, and mind. This type of painful memory can be like a movie with reruns playing over and over, never ending. Tragic moments may never fade, as in my case. An out of order death can shatter a heart at any moment, leaving scars forever… My life's worst impacts—my sister Martha who never saw her 25th birthday—my brother George, 36 years young, brutally murdered. The ultimate tragedy happened 35 years later! I buried my only child. Laura passed away in her sleep at 49 years young. My beautiful daughter's death created the worst pain imaginable—I have learned to live every day with a broken heart. With time and patience, these milestones in life will forever remain, bittersweet. I can't fix the brokenness—I can only get through it. Joy will continue to find me in my walks down memory lane, to once again run into those I've loved and lost.

Tragedy - My first impact

In the 50s and 60s, young adults knew living at home wasn't the "in" thing during the freedom era. My sister Martha and I married young, out of high school. Growing up, we hadn't become friends until we became mothers. We loved getting together with our toddlers, enjoying good conversation over morning coffee. I had one daughter and Martha had two, all close in age.

My first husband and I were busy remodeling our small house in the early '70s. During that time, Martha struggled in her marriage. Things began falling apart and her situation was irretrievable. There were issues her husband was unable to overcome. She once confided in me saying, "Someone at a party slipped a drug in my drink and I am not the same. Under certain lights I see things double, it never goes away." Martha sought help while her husband's family took her girls temporarily. It seemed at that point her hope and fight for life began eroding. Looking back, my sister struggled with severe depression. It was never shared with family but I could see it in her eyes. She often came to me when troubled—until it was to be—her last visit. That particular day, she seemed different, almost despondent. Being in my 20s, I was too young to see the signs. I tried cheering her up, letting her know things would get better. Words were of no help. Martha somehow created an impenetrable fortress, blocking all light from entering. This prevented the comfort and love of her family from reaching her. While busy making dinner, Martha quietly walked into the bathroom, swallowing all her newly prescribed antidepressants. Within 20 minutes she was rushed to the hospital, unable to survive the horrible ordeal. My beautiful sister died from loss of hope. Today, suicide is considered, "death of despair."

Martha will forever hold a place in our hearts, now filled with holes…I choose to treasure the good memories of my kind and generous sister. She was beautiful inside and out. My fond remembrances of Martha are shared throughout my stories, the bits and pieces of my life.

My second impact

"Georgie" was my big brother—there for me always. His name matured to "George" once he wore the navy uniform…The week before his horrific death, we had chatted by phone for quite a while. He was on the mend, recovering from a back injury. While putting an air conditioner in his bedroom window, one of his hands slipped. As he reached to grab for it, the force pulled his back out. After many weeks of recovery, he headed back to work that afternoon. Less than a week later, the nightmare began. George was a Massachusetts State Trooper, killed in the line of duty in 1983. He was doing a double shift for another Trooper who had called in sick. During a routine traffic stop, he was shot 7 times, left dying on the side of the road. The murderers shot another bullet into the tire of his cruiser to ensure their getaway…It took years before I was able to talk about that horrifying night without feeling a sense of panic.

When a loved one is taken away perilously, life is never the same for those left behind. George was 36 years old when he was killed, leaving behind a wife, three young children, his parents, and siblings. In my first book, great detail was written about George's last hours of life and the outrage this horrific killing left behind. My books of true stories reveal how my close-knit family had to overcome far too many tragedies.

It seems memories, as in my brother's murder, can be vivid with action and color, remaining this way for a lifetime. I believe in time it's our happier memories that help us let go of the darkest ones. George left behind a myriad of happy memories. Growing up, he was the kind of kid that any adult or parent would love to have called his or her own. Throughout his short life, those who knew him had the greatest respect and admiration. After all, he died a true hero.

***

Spring back in time with me to the summer of 1958…As all kids do, I remember seeing the world through curious eyes while seeking out joy in all that I did! Being an 8-year-old pesky sister of a 10-year-old brother, I worked hard for Georgie's approval. We both enjoyed sports, which included belonging to a neighborhood baseball team. My brother, being the oldest kid on the street, enjoyed having all the boys look up to him. With help from a neighboring school coach, Georgie gathered almost enough boys to put a team together. One more player was needed on the new "no name" team. The dilemma was he didn't want to ask his kid sister. His buddy, Billy, had a crush on me, and had no problem doing the asking. That day I happened to be hanging around. The team knew I played often enough to be a fairly good batter…Twisting my hair and hiding it under a baseball cap made me proud to be one of the boys on my brother's team. After all, I earned the reputation of being a tomboy since hanging out with them was my thing!

Another embedded memory was of a practice when our team pitcher became sick and I was asked to take his place. Just past the first inning, a batter hit a fast ball I never saw coming. Needless to say, it walloped my cheekbone narrowly missing my eye. The side of my face was black and blue, and my eye, swollen shut the next day. Even though my brother came to my rescue, he knew I wasn't a quitter. I was a team member and the only pitcher they had. The pain was worth it, we made the local paper, winning first place. Best of all, our team now had a name, the Red Wings. I still remember cutting out our team's picture from the front page of the local sports section. Seeing myself in a baseball cap with a name and numbered shirt reinforced my desire to remain in the boys club for as long as I could. The framed article hung on my bedroom wall for a few seasons. Once we moved to our new home, the article was put away and replaced with a picture of a handsome teenage boy who, by the way, was a pretty good kisser… My tomboy days were rapidly coming to an end.

My brother Georgie never had to say how proud he was after we won our games. I'd see it in his eyes or in his half smile after a win. Deep down I always knew my big brother would go to bat for his little sister—until that fatal day on the job in 1983—the night he died my hero.

Ironically that was who George Jr. was before his life ended in tragedy. After graduating from Marion High Catholic School, George joined the Navy and later, the Massachusetts State Police as a Trooper—to protect, defend, honor and serve.

The ultimate impact

From the time Laura was born, our lives became entwined in a way I never thought possible. A baby girl so precious and beautiful stole my heart forever. There isn't much that endures a lifetime like a mother and daughter connection. Along our journey, Laura had brought love and happiness, worry and sadness, friendship and pride. Laura came into her own as an adult. Determined and full of life, her impulsive and stubborn nature often took her on difficult paths. Whatever it was she put her mind to, she was all in doing it her way. The happiest times of her life were when her two children, John Jr. and Brooke, were born. Her goal was to be a good mother, especially when her children needed her most. She was a good friend to those needing advice and everyone loved her sense of humor. My daughter's quick wit often got a laugh out of me, not an easy feat when you're the serious type. During later years when her children had grown, Laura suffered from deep depression as did her father who died by suicide. This was a struggle for Laura. In her middle forties, she

9

developed several health issues. The fatal diagnosis was a rare form of pulmonary hypertension, with a five-year survival rate.

"Always in my heart—forever missed."

Memories of Bacon School

Chapter 2

Spiral back with me to September 1954, reliving a childhood memory.

My first year as a kindergartener brought new friends into my early life. The big red schoolhouse so elegantly displayed on top of Walnut Hill was built in a prestigious area of Natick. Parents throughout our neighborhood were anticipating another year of education for their youngsters. Population in the town during that era was just over 19,000, allowing fewer children per classroom. This type of education has always been every parent's dream. Small classes allow teachers to focus on students individually. As a kindergartener, all that attention wasn't to my benefit if I remember correctly. Nevertheless from there I went to Catholic school with nearly 50 children in a class…more in my next chapters.

It felt like a different world back in the day—neighbors were friendly and life seemed simpler. Many adults took considerable pride in being watchdogs, looking out for one another's children. Living in a quaint little town allowed parents to know most everyone. At one time, Natick had a great deal of open land, unlike today when buildings are being placed wherever there is space. Over the years our urban oasis has just about vanished. Wildlife has had to make adjustments, coexisting together in forests that are dwindling in size.

When it came to education growing up, I don't recall parents doing homework with us. We were mostly on our own, facing any and all consequences. In fact, due to strong discipline, kids back then outperformed today's young children in all subjects. There was far more expected of us. Rules were rules, and when we were asked to do something, we did it. For the most part, there were more children per family and parents were frugal. Today when parents ask kids to do something, they generally take their requests under consideration.

My first teacher at Bacon School was a delightful woman named Mrs. Gramzow. She'll always be remembered for helping me through tears of separation my first day. Her kind and gentle ways assured the class she was there to help with great listening ears. To balance that statement she would always say; "Every child deserves to be heard when appropriate." If memory serves me correctly, she had considerable patience with all the children. Her kindergarteners were her priority. She was unafraid of disciplining her kids when appropriate.

I recall a frightening instance never forgotten. During recess, a boy named Bobby took me aside and whispered, "There's a witch living in the nearby woods." He pointed out the window toward the woodlands, once called Barker's Woods. Part of the woods had wetlands and in the fall under controlled conditions, the firemen would burn down the bog for skating. Across from the pond was Walnut Hill School, still in existence today. It sits atop a steep hill where kids would go sledding and tobogganing.

Bobby said, "The witch only goes after girls! She captures and puts an 'evil spell' on them." Holding back tears, I asked what that meant and he sneered while saying, "You're next!" I didn't know what a "spell" was and yes, too frightened to ask. From that day forward, I'd peer out during recess and see smoke coming from the witches' chimney, wondering if I was next... No one could see the house deep in the woods, supporting Bobby's story. He was quite successful in scaring the girls and placing a spell on me!

As a youngster, I walked past these woods on my way home from school each day. I began refusing to walk without a parent or go skating or sledding with family. I'd either tell my mom it was too cold to walk, or I didn't feel good. Needless to say, between being afraid of the woods and the sleepless nights due to nightmares, my parents decided they'd had enough. They sat me down and asked what was wrong... While sobbing I said, "There's a spell on me, I'm afraid of the woods." After digging deeper and getting few answers, Dad grabbed his car keys and headed over to Bobby's house. The next day my mother coerced me into the car to confront my fear. She drove in the direction of the woods, turned in, and proceeded down a long driveway. We were about to meet the nice people who lived in the witch's house. When I saw the smoke and no signs of a witch, the nightmare was over. The next day back in school, Mrs. Gramzow not only had a private word with Bobby, she said to the children, "It was unacceptable behavior to tell lies and scare others." Back then, teachers had free reign on discipline and believe me, none of us were worse off for it. Bobby had to apologize and sit in the corner for a week.

By February, Bobby and I ended up being good friends again. On Valentine's Day when the kids dropped their cards in the fancy decorated box, Bobby left a red heart on my desk. It read, *"What did the stamp say to the envelope,"* on the bottom was written, *"I'm stuck on you!"* I remember this because once home, I placed that heart in my *"feelings box,"* given to me by my Aunt Floss. I saved that special valentine for years. How wonderful to look back and realize kids do get over spats far quicker than most adults.

I recall a change made to Bacon School while in kindergarten. There was a fire escape "tube" added, to safely evacuate those on the upper floor…Surely this is a fond memory for many adults that attended the school —it certainly was for me. Children were told they were not allowed to climb up the metal tube. Thing is, all we had to do was wait for weekends and summers to overrule. Kids made bets as to how far up they could climb. We'd each bring wax paper believing we could slide down faster than lightening. I rather doubt it made a difference. Most kids didn't make it to the top because it was too steep or dreadfully hot! Oftentimes when someone tried conquering the painful climb, a buddy would be on the lookout for police or a parent drive-by. This of course made for more excitement! Many of us went home with near first degree burns on our arms, hands and/or legs. It didn't take parents long to figure out what was happening. Nowadays, there'd be lawsuits! Regardless, kids will be kids, invariably ready for most any challenge when hanging with friends. There were days when it was over 100 degrees in that tube, but for kids it didn't matter. Believe me, I was burned by the challenge myself, many times!

It wasn't long before enough complaints were being made by parents, forcing changes to the fire escape. When school was out for summer, a cover was place at the bottom—made to keep kids out. This new safety feature only made it better for us. The cover came off when school began. The challenge was much more enjoyable in cooler weather, during vacations, and those early evenings when days grew longer.

The best part of those days at Bacon School was the memories and friends we made. Thanks to today's social media, many of us are back in touch…Recently a friend shared an old picture of our troop in Brownie uniforms in front of Bacon School. I remember feeling so proud wearing my uniform on days we had scout activities. We worked hard earning our badges and were excited for the things accomplished. Of course the best part of kindergarten? Waiting for the loud bell to sound at the end of the day!

Interesting facts about Bacon School

In more recent years, Natick has nearly doubled its population to over 35,000 in 2018. Bacon School was built in 1903 and after many generations of children educated there, it closed for demolition in 1976. Over the years, this distinctive building did have a few design changes to accommodate more children. Bacon School withstood 73 years of good and bad weather. Doors opened each and every year, integrating all those who were there to teach and learn.

I remember the day I pulled over to watch my old school being demolished. Sadly staring at the worn-down building with its broken windows, was another reminder of changing times and the old adage, nothing lasts forever... Despite this fact, the demolition of Bacon School couldn't tear down my fond recollections as I continue my journey.

The picture used in this story was taken from the
Natick playground
where Bacon School once stood - 2018

Mary's Catholic School Memories

Chapter 3

1955 - 1964

When recalling my past 60-plus years, I often ponder on how Mary survived those endless days in Catholic School. Flashbacks flow easily recalling her first day of school, walking into St. Patrick's elegant front entrance. How frightened she felt, meeting her first grade teacher, Sister Anita. The nun's voice was deep and intimidating, leaving Mary to wonder if her teacher was a man or woman. The only thing appearing feminine was the long black dress, adorned with a bib and large rosary beads that dangled from her neck. Sister Anita's stern, pumpkin-shaped face, along with her black and white outfit, was quite unnerving. Surely at 5 ½ years of age,

Mary didn't understand her anxious feelings exactly. She was told that nuns were sisters of God and she was to obey her teacher.

Being a nervous Nellie, Mary felt the urge to go, raising her hand asking to use the "girl's room." Sister Anita's answer was always, "not until recess." These persistent denials had been contributing factors to her many childhood bladder infections. Mary generally suffered this painful condition in silence. She recalls being reprimanded for her crocodile tears, giving reason and an excuse for Sister Anita to keep her back another year. This was a common practice back then. If children appeared immature, they were held back.

Although her name at home and outside of school was Molly, the nuns insisted she be called by her religious name, Mary. Mother Superior insisted upon children being called by their baptismal name and not their nicknames. Mary often wondered if other children who had attended Catholic School grappled with similar experiences. For the most part and over time, she learned to stand up for herself. She attributes much of her feisty attitude and inner strength to her well-disciplined upbringing. This also created her ability to face many losses and tragic events throughout her lifetime.

Another known fact…Students like Mary developed proper handwriting taught at Catholic schools. It was a must that children learn cursive. Mary still remembers that long ruler hanging over her hand every time she tried to write with her left hand. Mary believes she was born left-handed, however the first and second grade nuns insisted she learn to write with her other hand. The one positive thing that came out of that archaic way of thinking—Mary is now ambidextrous.

Over the next eight years, there were many walks across the street to St. Patrick's Church. This was a common occurrence before any religious holiday. During her first attendance in first grade, Mary learned that those two large closet-style boxes at the back of the church were called confessionals. There were two entrances on either side of the priest who remained hidden from view. Parishioners would wait their turn, before entering the small space. Once inside, there was little time to recall all the bad things we'd done to others, in order to be purified. Once the priest slid the small door open with a screen for blocking, the first thing we were taught to say was; *"Bless me father for I have sinned."* We then had to think about how many sins were committed, and when finished, our penance varied. Usually it was several Hail Mary's and Our Father's. Mary's brain would always draw a blank once inside the box, mainly due to fearing the wrath. It seemed she was always guessing as to how many lies she had told. Ironically guessing was a lie in itself. It's understandable why so many Catholics grew up with feelings of guilt. Over time, Mary believed any words spoken in the confessional were not as important as her daily actions. Her closeness with God came when she discovered private sessions with

Him on a one to one basis. This brought peace as she exposed more of what was in her heart during prayer.

On occasion, I've shared Mary's comical story of the morning her fourth grade class walked over to confession during Lent. Spring had arrived as the children prepared for the celebration of Easter. That morning there were two nuns watching over the large class. Once the children were seated in the pews, there was an eerie sound of silence, almost deafening. Mary began feeling anxious due to those unwelcoming noises coming from her stomach, those unwished-for rumbling sounds telling us we're hungry. There were at least five rows of children with one nun sitting in the first and the other in the last row. Mary sat somewhere in the middle. All of a sudden her stomach began to growl loudly, sounding exactly like a drawn-out angry cat. Both nuns began looking under the pews—to their left, right, all around—until they spotted Mary's red face. As much as she tried covering her mouth, she was unable to control her laughter. It became contagious amongst her classmates—they were in stitches… Needless to say, Mary had to be first in the confessional box and once back in class, she had to stay after school and write 500 times, *"I will not misbehave in church."*

As Mary blossomed in her last years of elementary school, the realization was setting in. Things had to change. She had grown tired of wearing the same old plaid uniform with green knee high socks, worn every day for years. By the time Mary reached seventh and eighth grade, she was totally bored with her look. Year after year, school pictures always came out looking the same, except for the different facial expressions. For some reason, Mary disliked her smile in seventh grade. Her teeth hadn't finished coming together. Yet her mother kept the unattractive picture hidden to keep Mary from tearing it up. Mary felt her teeth were too big for her face. Fortunately, by the time she was in high school, the other teeth fully developed, forcing them together. Back then fewer kids wore braces and when they did, they wore heavy metal smiles.

She decided one day to ask her mom for a new hairdo, since she would soon graduate from St. Patrick's School. Mary's mom brought her to a hairstylist, giving Mary a shorter hairdo which transformed her into a teenager. It was quite bouffant, even for Mary. After leaving the hair salon, she tried pushing it down. The next morning she added a small bow, hoping the nuns would approve. She believed this would save her from the embarrassment of being scolded in front of the class. Just as Mary suspected, on the day of pictures, in front of a class of 50 students, Sr. Mary Ellen made her stand up.

With a stern face, Sister Mary Ellen insisted, "no pictures until you comb that hair out!" She continued, "If you don't do this during recess, get your coat and go home."

Sister Mary Ellen then told Mary to meet her in the hallway. It was there she insisted Mary also wipe the rouge off her face. Unbeknownst to the Sister, Mary's cheeks were completely flushed from being humiliated in front of the class—she wore no make-up… This may not have been considered a crime, however by today's standards, it was abusive treatment.

At this point, Mary finally decided to stand up for herself, which in retrospect is how she survived Catholic School. During recess, she grabbed her coat and walked out the large front doors of the school. Once on the sidewalk, Mary realized what she had done.

Mary then cautioned herself by saying; "Oh God, where will I go?"

She knew there would be just as much punishment going home as going back to apologize. Her next thought was to run in the opposite direction, to her grandmother's house. Mary felt this to be her best option…Her grandmother was a big woman in her early 80s and Mary relied on her for protection. As she walked up the hill, every disquieted thought played out in her mind. Her grandmother, "Wawa," had always been her go-between and this time was no different. It didn't take long before her dad came grumbling through the front door. Wawa not only stuck up for her, she stood in front of Mary with arms stretched out—the rest is history!

If for no other benefit, attending Catholic school just may have afforded Mary a ticket to heaven. A priest once told her, as long as she stays on the high road in prayer, she had a guarantee. Mary truly believes that as bad as things were at times, these "abuses" helped her develop an undeniable strength within.

In her last year at St. Patrick's, Mary had a wonderful teacher, Sr. Eileen Francis. Mary had such admiration for this beautiful nun who not only understood her; she stood up and protected Mary. Her gentle kindness gave Mary the spiritual strength and inspiration to carry her into the next phase of life after graduation.

————— · —————

We don't develop courage by being happy every day. We develop it by surviving difficult times and challenging adversity.

Barbara De Angelis

Feelings Placed in a Box

Chapter 4

Early in the morning Mary awoke quickly, in hopes of feeling better. Peering out the window from her bed, she noticed a blinding snow squall. A winter storm was forecasted with high winds and over a half foot of snow. As she approached the window, her eyes stared at the ground, only to discover no accumulation. Disappointed and tired from lack of sleep, she knew it would be difficult sitting in her second grade classroom. For Mary, feelings of disappointment emerged. During the night her lower tummy ached and for that reason, she prayed for several feet of snow by morning. She needed to find a reason to stay home from school. As she began making her bed, Mary wondered if Mother would send her without a fever. As mention in the last chapter, first grade was hard on Mary. Mostly due to frequent belly aches and the teacher not allowing her to leave class to use the girl's room. She often wondered why it was only her needing to use the lavatory more so than the other children.

Mary came downstairs for breakfast and contemplated whether to tell her mother about another tummy ache during the night. She wanted so badly to stay home. Mother always sent her kids to school unless they had a temperature. Mary felt she'd be out of luck and so without a word, she marched back up upstairs. She needed to draw another sad face, placing it in her new box. In spite of her discomfort and fears, this brave little girl went off to school.

With one older brother, two younger sisters, and two brothers in diapers, her mom was overworked. They lived in a small New England style Cape and as nice as it was, the family had one bathroom. Mother was always organized, right down to the times children needed baths. Saturday night was set aside for the girls and Sunday evenings the boys. The girls always bathed around the same time as, "*The Lawrence Welk Show*." It was like clockwork hearing the music while playing with the bubbles. We loved sticking them on each other's faces making beards.

Being the oldest of the girls, Mary began expressing her dislike being in the same tub with her younger sisters. The youngest still liked playing in the dirt while Mary managed to stay clean for the most part. When mother ran the bathwater, she always added Mr. Bubble, believing it would kill any bacteria…Once Mary turned 8, she began asking to bath in those bubbles without her sisters. As many times as she expressed her feelings, mom's answer was always, "Sharing is the way it has to be living in a small house with a big family."

Mary's "feelings box" was nearly 50 years old. It had a lock with a small ancient-looking key. The pretty box was made of dark mahogany wood that was not only beautiful to Mary, it was special. That's why it was important for her to keep it hidden so that Mary's sisters couldn't find the box or key. It was a unique gift from her Auntie Floss. When giving it to Mary, she said, "When something hurts and you're feeling sad, write your feelings on paper and place them in your special box. And remember, safeguard it so it will always be there keeping you and your 'feelings' safe."

Months after Mary's aunt died, she came across a beautiful picture of Auntie Floss in the attic. She thought if she placed her picture in the "feelings box," she'd be able to see and talk with her, helping Mary through all her troubles.

Mary had made a good decision that morning. Her anxious feelings calmed down once she scribbled something on a scrap of paper and placed it in her special box. It helped give her courage after leaving her "feelings" with Auntie Floss. Once dressed for school, she did her best to put on a smile as she headed out the door. Of course she wasn't in class an hour when she felt the urge to use the girl's lavatory. As always, she continued to get the same old, "wait till recess" answer from the teacher as she sat with her tummy ache. This physical pain seemed to become a part of Mary's life. As she walked home from school after a long day, she decided to tell her Mom about the pain in her tummy. Being so young, Mary didn't know how to explain what was happening.

Just as she got off the school bus, Mary noticed a lot of commotion going on. It wasn't long before she put the pieces together. Their family dog had gotten out of their fenced-in yard again. Rudy had chased another car causing an accident in front of their house. Thank goodness the two elderly people were driving slowly. Rudy had forced the car into a tree causing the gentleman's face to hit the steering wheel resulting in a serious nose bleed. When father got home, the decision was made that Rudy, who was often mistaken for Lassie, needed to live on a farm. Dad explained to the children that Rudy was the kind of dog who needed to run and was unhappy fenced in. The children were sad and upset having to say goodbye to Rudy, who was a big part of their family. With all the excitement, this distracted Mary from thinking about her tummy pain.

Once dinner time rolled around, everyone began telling their stories of the day. After dessert, the family sat together to watch their favorite TV show. Of course back in the 1950s, there were only three channels to choose from. If a channel needed changing, someone had to get up, turn the knob and adjust the rabbit ears… Before going to bed that night, Mary made the decision to say something to her mother. Once together in her parent's bedroom, Mother had asked Mary what was wrong. Feeling embarrassed, she wanted to tell her but words wouldn't come. The tears began rolling down her cheeks, and Mary could only say her tummy hurt. Her mother softly spoke, "Mary honey, you just have a nervous stomach. A good night sleep will help things calm down and you'll feel much better in the morning." Mother didn't know the extent of her daughter's suffering. For Mary, when her tummy ached at night, she'd be too bashful and afraid to tell anyone, shedding many quiet tears. That's when she found herself using her "feelings box," placing one note on top of another.

Mary's mother was now beginning to worry about her daughter. Her once vivacious little girl, who used to laugh and interact with everyone, had becoming withdrawn. It was time to make a doctor's appointment. After the tests were completed, the doctor spoke in great length with Mary's mother. Dr. Burke felt the biggest culprit was her bathing situation. The tests concluded Mary was having chronic and painful urinary tract infections.

The doctor said to Mary, "It's time for you to take showers only. No more bathing in Mr. Bubble!" Mary was excited to hear she no longer had to sit in the bathtub with her sisters. With treatment and changes, her symptom resolved and she was able to be that fun loving tomboy once again. In just a short time, her mother noticed her daughter was belly laughing and socializing with the neighborhood kids once again. Most importantly, Mary looked forward to the upcoming summer activities which included vacationing with family.

Even though summertime flew by quickly, the season didn't end well for Mary. She had been watching her older brother and his friends tackle a very large hornets' nest in a tree. It was way too close to their fort they had spent weeks building. Even though Mary felt she was standing far enough away from the nest, the boys proceeded to pitch a pointed handle that once held an old shovel into the nest of bees. The boys took off like a flash going in one direction while the bees swarmed in the direction of Mary. She couldn't run fast enough and ended up with many stings. Her Mom comforted her, giving her a cool shower and yes, without her sisters. She also applied plenty of calamine lotion, even though the bee stings hurt like crazy. Mary, being far too familiar with pain, found that being stung many times wasn't as bad as the tummy aches she endured.

Other than an occasional check-in to share her happy thoughts with her aunt, Mary rarely needed her treasured "feelings box"…

Looking back on my life, I often fall back on this quote by, Walter Mosley: ***"If it wasn't for bad luck, I'd have no luck at all"***

Pressing the Recall Button

Chapter 5

Those wild moments at Girl Scout camp—a memory in need of a recall! There I was with bags in hand, eager to have my first experience away from home. My insides were bursting with excitement and readiness. While waving goodbye to my mother, anxiety began to take hold. My 8-year-old brain mused while in overdrive, trying to calm the butterflies in my tummy. Thoughts poured out: "Mother, I'll be in the woods for a week, who will protect me from the wild animals? I can't call home, there's no phone!" She responded with affection and love, "I have faith that God and his helpers at Camp Nacochwa will take good care of you." Although I felt better, these worried thoughts weighed heavily—until being happily distracted by friends eager to go camping.

After hitting the recall button again, I closed my eyes... There in my view was a yellow school bus. As I focused in, the leaders and the troop were being dropped off near the woods. All together, we walked briskly down a sandy path.

I noticed the wild berry bushes and trees lining the trails. My first real sighting was the 6x9 tents we'd all be sleeping in. The dark green canvases tied to heavy metal stakes all positioned atop five wooden decks, arranged in circular fashion. Off in a distance was the dining hall with a large bell hanging from wooden rafters. The loud bong alerted everyone to the hall for signing in, meals, and activities. The cabin had a worn wooden exterior which blended nicely against the backdrop of the tall pine trees. The large stone fireplace was the source of heat for all who entered. When the fire wasn't going, the opening was big enough to walk inside where the wood is placed. Next to the main entrance was a door to a comfy restroom, used by camp councilors only. We were given a map detailing where the outhouses were. What an eye opener for a kid... Looking down that deep hole surely must have sent me home constipated! I'm sure there was no getting up at night when nature called.

The view of the lake from the open porch was tantalizing. After lunch and a meeting at the hall, our next activity was swimming lessons. Once back in the tent, I began the difficult task of putting on my bathing suit inside my sleeping bag. I refused to change in front of seven girls! By the end of the week, I'd gotten pretty good at it. The girls were laughing and singing as we all headed down the path to the beach. There on the dock stood a lifeguard with a whistle signaling to the girls to climb on the dock. She hollered, "Each camper must jump off one by one to begin swimming lessons." While waiting my turn, I stood in the water thigh high, only to feel mushy disgusting leaves under foot. While waiting for the last of the girls to jump in, I felt something attach to my leg. After coming out of the water, I looked down in horror! There stuck to my leg were a couple of plump maroon colored worms. I began screaming unable to get them off. A maintenance man nearby came to my rescue. He lit a cigarette, took a few puffs to get it hot and proceeded to encourage these bloodsuckers to detach on their own. The leeches didn't need to be plucked off, the heat from the cigarette worked. I ran to the hall where the nurse gave me first aid. "That's it!" I snarled at the nurse and continued, "I'm done with camp, the lake and swimming lessons!" Nearby, a sympathetic counselor named Virginia took me under her wing. Otherwise I would have walked all the way home. Within days, she got me back in the water, jumping off the dock and teaching me the proper swim strokes. On the last day of camp, I actually won a blue ribbon in a swimming contest.

The next fiasco came on the second night when Jane decided to rescue her marshmallow that had fallen into the campfire. Her hand sustained first and second degree burns which ended her days at camp. That was our last night for making s'mores. Nevertheless we had lots of laughs sitting around the campfire singing songs. My most memorable, "*Make New Friends and Keep the Old*," one is silver and the other is gold. Another was, *Sing High! Sing Low!* A few years later, after my camping experience, a funny song came out about camp... *Hello Muddah, Hello Faddah*— 1963—by Allen Sherman... Listening, and identifying with the song on YouTube, still brings fond memories and laughter!

Back at camp, the distant whistle blew for the third night. By then we knew what to do. It was ten o'clock, time for our beauty sleep. There'd be no more chatting, joking or laughing. That night seemed colder than the one before. Everyone was zipped up nestled in their sleeping bags. Once in mine, I felt itchy all over and began scratching every inch of my body. I was being eaten alive by more bloodsucking monsters.., mosquitos! Between the discomfort and being homesick, my eyes welled with tears. I silently repeated over and over, "Girl Scouts are brave," until sleep finally occurred.

With one eye open, I knew morning had arrived. The brilliant sun peeked through the forest while shadows were being cast on the screen section of our tent. After taking a deep breath, I dressed before the others awoke and hunted down the nurse. Virginia was finishing breakfast when she saw me running toward her. She remained calm noticing the bites and blotches of poison ivy. Virginia slathered me in calamine lotion and promised things would get better. I was pink all over! Although I participated in most activities that day, feelings of homesickness always simmered below the surface…Looking back through my writing, the pieces finally came together as to why I had difficulty being away from home. Months before camp, the little girl I once was, lost a baby sister to pneumonia. This loss was the connection to much of my sadness.

With the battery dying—there was little time left using the recall button…In ending another recall, I continue to learn that our lifelong journey is full of all kinds of happenings…As Steven Preece once said: *"Life is a journey of experiences, some good—some bad and some we choose to forget!"* When it comes to camping, I've learned over time, it isn't for everyone… For me, I'm a cottage-by-the-sea type of gal. As for my first experience at camping, I'll always be grateful for the early adventure. Camping with the Girl Scouts helped me grow in self-confidence and independence. I also discovered lasting friendships. Most importantly, a certain counselor caught a glimpse of sadness underneath my exterior and came to my rescue. My mother was right about one of God's helpers being there. Virginia encouraged me to find joy in every undertaking. She also helped me to find courage to overcome many obstacles during a crucial time in my life.

THE GIRL SCOUT PROMISE

On my honor, I will try:
To serve God and my country,
To help people at all times,
And to live by the Girl Scout Law

THE GIRL SCOUT LAW

I will do my best to be honest and fair, friendly and
helpful,
considerate and caring, courageous and strong, and
responsible for what I say and do, and to respect
myself and others,
respect authority, use resources wisely,
make the world a better place, and be a sister to every
Girl Scout.

Authors Unknown

The Hobo Who Found Trouble on Halloween

Chapter 6

Abrisk autumn weekend was predicted with no signs of rain. Children were making plans for their big Saturday night event. Many already decided on their Halloween costumes. Mary was a third grader with an adventurous nature. Since she was one of a large family, with an older brother and four younger siblings, her parents couldn't afford to buy costumes. Most of their costumes were handmade or hand-me-downs. It wasn't unusual in the mid-1900s for mothers to be creative in making children's outfits for trick-or-treat. In fact there were plenty of white sheets to make oodles of ghosts and goblins back in the day!

Being the tomboy she was, Mary loved dressing like a boy. Both she and her brother Georgie were overly excited to see their costumes. Mother was putting the last touches on her creations, making Mary's hobo costume along with Georgie's black cape. He decided to be the character

"Zorro," needing a cape, a face mask and a sword. A friend lent him the mask and sword to complete the look. As brothers do, Georgie loved scaring his younger sisters. Halloween was generally the best time to spook us when least expected. He loved jumping out of a closet or from behind a bush wearing a scary mask and a dark ski hat. George was famous for inflicting fear after dark. He got a kick out of torturing his sisters!

It wouldn't be long before the neighborhood kids would once again gather together to ring doorbells, anticipating their treats. The more boys Mary trick or treated with, the happier she was, especially when she had the most candy. Sometimes her mom would catch Mary double dipping just to beat her brother. As Georgie got older, he was allowed out longer to travel further from the neighborhood with friends. Funny thing, no matter how much candy everyone got, Mother found ways to throw away as much as possible.

Mary discovered early on that two of the girls in her neighborhood were bullies. Mary didn't like conflict that often happened when she was with them. Peggy was the worst! She would find ways to take their mutual friend Kathy to her house, excluding Mary. It's not uncommon to see one pushed aside when three girls get together. Being a child, the "three's a crowd" situation can sometimes be another hard lesson learned. However, the school of hard knocks is where problems become an opportunity for growing emotionally.

To Mary's delight, she had discovered there were more boys in the neighborhood than girls. She often gravitated to them as she liked playing boys' sports. Hanging with them got her into ball games when there weren't enough players. Mary also recalled a lucky break she once had. Her older brother allowed her to go inside his shabby club house. The sign outside read; "No Girls Allowed." Mary felt privileged to be the only girl permitted when no one was around!

When Saturday morning arrived, Mother noticed the neighborhood kids were out and about early. It was the morning of Halloween and they were already buzzing around awaiting the fun-filled night. With one eye open, Mary realized the best holiday of the year, besides Christmas, was finally here. After breakfast she was looking for something to do to pass time. She understood the importance of behaving on Halloween. Trouble often found her without looking!

Across the street she noticed a babysitter watching over the two boys who lived there. One of them was her 9-year-old friend Jack, who was a year older than Mary. They loved racing their bikes around and playing outdoors together. That particular day while Jack's babysitter was making cupcakes, she discovered there wasn't enough sugar to make the frosting. The babysitter decided to take Jack's younger brother to the store. This left Jack alone for 20 minutes with instructions to stay inside and watch TV. While the treats were cooling, he became bored and needed a distraction to keep from devouring the cupcakes.

After the babysitter drove away, Jack yelled across to Mary, "Hey, come over for a cupcake, Jill will be right back. She said it was OK."

Once inside, Mary could not resist the delightful aroma of chocolate coming from the kitchen. Jack ran ahead, opened the fridge and grabbed the whipped cream. He took a knife from the draw, cut out the top center of two warm cupcakes and began squirting the cream inside. He finished by placed the tops back on…Wow, Mary was blown away! The cream filled cupcakes were the most amazing snack she had ever tasted…Better than the Hostess filled ones!!!

After Jack put all the evidence back, he asked Mary to check out his erector set that he was building upstairs in his room. Mary was hesitant but was reassured by Jack that the babysitter would be right back. When they got to his bedroom, Jack told her the erector set was in the closet. Unbeknownst to Mary, Jack had locked his bedroom door. He opened the closet door, put on the light and after several minutes of coaxing Mary in, he shut the door. She became frightened and reached to open the door only to find it locked! Her heart was beating fast as she began to cry. Jack now scared, hoisted himself up to the top shelf and stayed there. Mary started yelling but no one could hear. She was panic-stricken as tears streamed down her face!

It seemed like forever before Mary and Jack finally heard the babysitter's loud, firm voice, "What's going on? Why is this door locked?" She heard Mary say the closet door was locked and knew she couldn't get into the room!"—Real trouble begins…

They both began hearing faint sounds of sirens. Jack whispered, "See I told you we'd be rescued." Mary began to feel her heart settle down until she realized her parents would not only hear the firetrucks coming but would see the commotion. "Oh no!" she said, "My parents are across the street!" All she could think about was her punishment for misbehaving. Mary's eyes filled as she thought, "no trick or treating for me. My friend Jack pulled the biggest trick ever and I'll be the one punished!" She began crying....

Sure enough, after a lot of pandemonium, a fireman came in through the window using the ladder truck to reach them. He opened both doors saving the day, at least for Jack. Now that Mary was free she thought of her hobo costume and realized she just might be wearing it permanently! The short walk to her house was torture. Just as she imagined, her parents were waiting with angry faces. She was sent to her room and told to stay there.

As day turned to dusk, Mary's parents understood that what happened to their daughter was a frightening situation. After talking it over, her parents realized nothing bad had happened and it was a learning experience for Mary. They felt because it was a rather traumatic event, Mary would never forget that particular Halloween.

At the end of the day, Mary's parents reached a decision. While the children were putting on their costumes, Mother went into the kitchen where Mary was drying the dishes. She had given her daughter a hug with permission to go trick or treating with her friends. Mary was not only the happiest hobo ever, she told her parents she would never let trouble find her again!

The Last Hayride
Chapter 7

Another trip down memory lane brought me to the days of those delightful hayrides. It also evoked one of my childhood traumas. My first recall was of Mr. Brooks who lived nearby. He had a modest home and enough land to house two horses in a small barn. I once believed Mr. Brooks' unapproachable demeanor and grumpiness to be who he was. Most neighborhood kids had similar feelings along with a few harrowing experiences. Especially when we'd get caught feeding his animals through the fence. Although fascinated with these large horses, my best friend Barbie and I were too afraid to get close to the hoofed animals or their owner. Nevertheless, we were delighted when Barbie's mother, our Girl Scout leader, had arranged for the troop to go on a hayride.

It was fall harvesting time and the nights were cooling down. The day of the hayride, I said to Barbie, "Let's go to the candy store and pick up a bunch of those one-cent fireballs. Jack and Billy will be hiding behind the trees when the wagon passes their house. We can toss one to each as a signal to jump on the wagon, hiding them under the hay!" Having much more insight than I, Barbie quickly replied, "Let's not!!! We could get kicked off near the dark woods where that witch lives." None of us forgot that scary story that spread around in kindergarten about the witch that lived in the nearby woods.

As daylight began to fade, the girls gathered at the school parking lot. One after another began jumping for joy as the wagon drew near. The sounds of bells jingling, the clip clop of horse's hoofs on the pavement could be heard. The old timber framed wagon filled with fresh hay turned in to the school parking lot. Sitting up front and holding the rein was a burly looking man, Mr. Brooks. He was wearing an oversized plaid coat and a rumpled hat over his straggly white hair. He reined in his two best friends—old Tom and Bessy the mare—until the horses stopped, snorted and shook their heads with pride. Tom appeared much older than Bessy. He was both enormous and strong looking, surely a handsome bay in his time. The elderly gentleman once told my dad that Tom worked the farm but better enjoyed pulling the wagon full of jovial kids excited to be with friends.

After jumping on and finding a comfy spot in the hay-packed wagon, the playful journey began. There was chatting and giggling and some of us hung over the sides feeling a sense of freedom. The wagon descended slowly down the street heading for the center of town. We waved to those walking along the sidewalks as the wagon headed for the winding back roads toward Sunshine Dairy. As the horses began the steep climb, there was a distinct odor of a barn nearby. It was a reminder that in spite of that nasty smell delicious ice cream was close by. Once we passed the barn filled with cows, we reached our final destination, the ice cream stand. Not only was it the best around, all dairy products were made and packaged right on the property. In the mid-1900s Sunshine Dairy not only sold ice cream in stores, they had several trucks delivering fresh milk in glass bottles to homes throughout the surrounding towns.

Darkness fell upon us as we made the trip back. The girls were much more subdued on the ride home. As the wagon approached the schoolyard, parents were seen patiently waiting. As I hopped off the wagon, I ran up front to hand Mr. Brooks a thank you note my mother made me write. However, on my own volition, I gave him my leftover fireballs, which made him smile.

As time marched on, I barely took notice of Mr. Brooks and his horses. Our family moved to a bigger house closer to town. Occasionally I'd hear the familiar sounds of hoofs hitting the pavement, as the horse-drawn wagon passed by. One particular evening, my older brother and I were leaving the library when we spotted Mr. Brooks heading home from a hayride. He was alone with his two best friends pulling the wagon. After what seemed a short time, we saw police cruisers heading in the same direction. Once we got within view, we noticed the police lights and Mr. Brooks wagon tilted on its side. One of the lanterns on the front was out. Georgie and I started running toward the scene. We spotted old Mr. Brooks on the ground in a sitting position. He said to the officer, "I don't want an ambulance, please, someone help my Tom." My brother Georgie noticed the damaged car that backed into the horse and wagon. At the time, the police were questioning the driver. I ran over to Tom to see what was wrong. I was horrified! It was an image never forgotten. Under the streetlight, Tom had a huge gash with his insides hanging out. He could barely stand on his front left leg. I still recall how helpless and frightened I felt.

Police officers told us to head home or stand behind a tree for safety. We didn't understand why at the time, but we did as told and went behind a large oak tree. All of a sudden two loud shots rang out. My brother said, "Molly, they shot Tom." This was the first time we had ever heard gun shots. The impact of seeing and hearing this was tough on a 10 and 13-year-old. No one explained why Tom had to be shot at the scene. Later we were told shooting a horse was a way of putting them down, perfectly legal back then. The teenager who sped out of his driveway in reverse never saw the horses…It was dark and there were no lights on the sides of the wagon.

Reflecting back, many things can shake us to the core. I remember how badly I felt for Tom and his owner. Surely Mr. Brooks had a heavy heart after losing his best friend. Following the accident, there were no hayrides to be seen.., no one knew what happened to Mr. Brooks. Years later, I learned the teen driving the car that fateful night never got over it. He drank a lot over his adult years, passing away before his time. As difficult as this was to witness, I believe these adversities over a lifetime provide us the opportunity to develop resilience. There is a saying, "If it doesn't kill you, it will make you stronger." We also know there are limits. One can only hope that once we come face to face with adversity and go through it, our strength will be realized, allowing us to focus on the positives.

Georgie Porgie

Chapter 8

When recalling those classic nursery rhymes, so many come to mind. Being a mighty Brownie in first grade, I call to mind the times our troop had to sing and act out, *"I'm a Little Teapot."* Can't believe we all went along with being tea pots short and stout... *"Georgie Porgie"* was one my brother Georgie detested most. Thanks to him, our grandfather was called "Alfie," the rest of us followed suit. I remember a time when Alfie pulled on one of Georgie's large ears reciting, *"Georgie Porgie pudding and pie, kissed the girls and made him cry, when the boys came out to play, Georgie Porgie ran away."* Of course I was more than happy to memorize that one! Trouble was, I wasn't allowed to vocalize this outdoors. My mother threatened, "Molly, if one of his friends catch wind of this, Georgie could be teased. And yes, you'd be in trouble!" Nowadays, that nursery rhyme would bring about a class action lawsuit for bullying or sexual harassment by the ACLU. Who was this

Georgie Porgie anyway? From my research, no one seems to know its origin.

I admit to feeling proud whenever my older brother looked out for me. My dad once said, "When Georgie was six, he took your little hand and walked you down the narrow road from your grandparent's farm. Once we realized he was taking you too far, we called out frantically. Georgie was preoccupied after seeing a pickup truck coming speedily up the road. That's when he dragged you lickety-split off the street, both falling on the grass laughing…From my prospective, I knew he'd always be your protector, at least through elementary school."

Coming from a family of seven, my oldest brother George was the first born with six siblings trailing behind. I was the oldest of the girls, two and a half years younger than my brother. When it came to influencing our younger siblings, we were a hard act to follow. Unbeknownst to us at the time, we had been setting examples. Obviously there were some things we wish they didn't see, hear or do. Kids imitate others, much like the primate species—monkey see monkey do…Growing up I often wondered why the two of us were sent to Catholic School and the other four to public schools. It's obvious there were high expectations placed on the two oldest. Our parents let their guard down with the others. Reflecting back, we did have a great deal of sway on our siblings. However, much of our behavior was generally positive, around the youngsters.

As time passes, there are many moments of reflection. I once said to George, "If only it were possible to be born *old* first, allowing our mistakes to be corrected over a lifetime." How amazing it would be to make changes for the better. Thing is, we can only connect the dots from our past, not in the unseen future. The cycle of life brings with it new beginnings, allowing no one to return and make changes. Our past is the only place we can learn and draw upon.

When I reflect on the years growing up with my late brother, I recall a rather tall handsome kid who was truly a hard act to follow. He may have been on the skinny side but with the help of his dad, he learned the importance of exercise. George was goal oriented, and consistently stayed the course no matter what he was trying to accomplish. It wasn't until he became a young man in his early 20s that he filled out handsomely—and yes, he grew into his ears. He was greatly admired by his sisters and brothers who looked up to him throughout his short life. George was a positive role model to all who knew him during his brief time on earth.

In terms of children, we did plenty of nonsense stuff that sometimes made my parents cringe, especially when we were making crazy decisions and doing embarrassing things. As a kid I once said to myself, "If I put my feet out the window in the middle of winter, maybe pneumonia would set in and there would be no school for a week." It didn't take long before I tested that theory. There I was, my feet dangling out, catching the snowflakes. Having my bed close to the window made it all too easy. Trouble was, the pain was setting in, my toes stung and I could barely move them. Before long, my feet started rejecting my nonsensical idea. That's when common sense kicked in. I pulled my bitterly cold feet in, studied until midnight, and headed off to school the next day.

Before moving to our family's dream home, I shared a bedroom in a small Cape-style home with my two younger sisters, Martha and Sue. Georgie's bedroom was directly across from ours on the second floor. I recall his record player with an old-style plug attached to it. It had cardboard over the two prongs and for some reason, it wasn't plugged in. Inside was a 45 rpm record, ready to be played. To this day, I still have a vivid memory of Elvis Presley's record, *"Hound Dog."* I believe on the other side was, *"Don't Be Cruel."* The picture on the black record label was a white hound dog with a phonograph. In 1956, these songs gave Elvis his biggest success on record…Being the self-determined sister that took chances, I plugged in the record player, knowing Georgie wasn't home. It was the beginning of a nightmare, like the 4th of July gone wrong! Sparks flew everywhere as I was jolted and thrown back—yikes! Talk about a close call and a "Bless me Father," moment! The good news is I don't recall my brother being mad at me. Surely he and my parents were grateful I was alive and the house didn't burn down.

After moving to our new place, our Christmases seemed to get better with time. Around 12 years old, I had asked for a portable record player under the tree…There it was, white with black trim, a long handle to carry, and it was lightweight. Plugging it in for the first time helped me overcome that shocking fear…By then I was earning my own money babysitting, and had a collection of my own 45s purchased at Woolworth's. All the songs were from the 60s. One of my favorites was Connie Francis's "*Where the Boys Are.*" How intoxicating it was standing in front of the mirror, with hairbrush in hand, pretending it was a microphone. I would lip synch the words as if being her, the beautiful and famous singer. There above my head was a pull-chain light and though I only had two minutes of fame under it, I still remember that mind-blowing feeling! Whenever I let out a few notes, laughter would erupt from somewhere in the house! I must admit, the only note I was able to carry was a B-flat. Lip synching became my only option. I remember a time when Georgie barged into my room. He caught me doing my Connie Francis act, laughing hysterically! Another one of my many blushing moments…

In my early teens, privacy was most important. My bedroom was padlocked due to two curious sisters thinking my room was the Goodwill warehouse—clothes free for the taking. Georgie was happy having his own room and delighted that his sisters had no interest in his apparel. Mark and John, being the youngest, were too young and only interested in their toy car Hot Wheels collection…Having my own bedroom felt like a small piece of heaven. Closing the door and shutting out the world was needed now and again. As small as it was, I was grateful.

As I complete this story filled with fond memories, I'll forever think of my brother as my protector…Always loved, never forgotten and forever missed… It's been 36 years since his death—he was 36 years old when murdered.

May God rest his soul and may our family one day be together in that truly peaceful place.

———————

Trooper George L. Hanna—February 26th—End of Watch—A True Hero.

In Loving Memory of my brother,

Trooper George L. Hanna

Happy Times on Walnut Hill

Chapter 9

Before the moving truck arrived, the children began pestering and pulling at Mother's apron strings, pleading to see their new home. Mary joined in by saying, "Mom, I promise to keep the other kids quiet and out of your hair. Please, I can't wait!" Mother knew this to be a tall order for her daughter. In just a few short months she would have her 10th birthday. Being the oldest girl, Mary was quite mature for her age. She'd taken on various responsibilities and at times more than she could handle. Being a determined child, she managed to get first dibs on her bedroom of choice. This would be a new passage for Mary.

After lunch, Mother finished cleaning the kitchen and began maneuvering her children in the direction of the station wagon. The kids were restless and overjoyed as they ran out the door. The movers finished packing the truck filled with boxes and furniture. Mary heard the large bulky doors slam shut as they prepared to follow the family to their new home on Walnut Hill. Off they went in their 1955 black Dodge station wagon, headed to the home that would be their last as a family together.

No sooner had they pulled in the driveway when the children began acting out in a frenzy. During the '50s there were no seat belts allowing parents to harness kids in place. My parents knew it was hard controlling us at times, especially when we were psyched—3-year-old John began chiming in by covering his ears and screaming for everyone to stop. Mother compared the excitement to the young teens screaming at an Elvis concert…Mary sat up front rolling her eyes saying, "As soon as this car stops, I'm out, beating everyone!" The others emerged from the vehicle, shoving one another in an attempt to race ahead of their big sister. The oldest boy, George, toppled out the rear window, trying to get in on the game…

Almost knocking down one of the movers, Mary made it inside, getting her first peak. Her face froze in awe, as if she'd just entered the White House. Mary gulped and said, "look how high and fancy these ceilings are." She then stated, "Yikes, we must be rich!" Mary didn't stick around for an answer—way too busy running from room to room. She pretended it belonged to a movie star. She couldn't wait to tell her friends and family she now had three toilets instead of one! From the upstairs, Mary heard her dad say, "Wow, I finally have my own throne!"

It wasn't long before the children spotted small white buttons on the walls in several rooms. Instead of asking, they began pushing them. To their mother's amazement and gratitude, they weren't working. Mother was thankful to learn most of the wires had been disconnected. Being the inquisitive one, Mary couldn't let anything go. She asked questions about these buttons and more. Her mother said, "The people that owned this house once had maids living on the third floor. When a family member needed to call a maid, they'd push one of the white buttons and one would come down the back stairs." She also stated, "The reason for two pantries off the kitchen was for the butler to store and prepare food in one, while the other was used to store fancy dishes. In between the pantries was a small passageway. A sliding door was used to transfer items from one to the other, keeping guests from seeing the servants."

Several of the rooms had the most elegant built-ins. Another of Mary's discoveries was the pocket doors used to shut off the living room from the dining area. "Wow, these doors are heavy," she said. Mary was also delighted with the room her dad would use as his new office. It had a thick door to keep any noise out of his space. This pleased everyone because the television in the living room would be far enough away, bringing peace to their new home.

When anyone came to the front door, the charming stained glass accent windows always resulted in compliments. Walking into the foyer brought feelings of warmth, with its stylish gas fireplace wrapped in small glistening sapphire tiles. To the left was an elegant mahogany staircase, leading up to the second floor. The woodwork in the home was ostentatious with both small and large columns. The magnificent designs would be hard to replicate today. In the kitchen was a door with back stairs leading to the second and third floor. Unfortunately for Mother, it was no longer being used by maids. She often spoke of the history that came with the house. On occasion Mother would say, "if only walls could talk."

Taking the back stairs, Mary quickly ran the three flights wondering what it would be like to live in the maid's quarters. She discovered three rooms all beautifully wallpapered. There was one in particular, where a breathtaking feeling came over her—surely due to the hot attic and running the stairs! Yet as Mary stood there, she knew this was the bedroom she would call her own. It was quite small and cozy, away from everyone else. Sleeping with her two sisters in the same room was officially over.

After arranging the furniture in her bedroom, Mary wanted to begin decorating the back of her door with 45 record sleeves. Her mother gave her fresh bedding with a beautiful orchid colored bedspread matching the pink and purple flowers in the wallpaper. Using scotch tape and her father's stapler, she hung up the sleeves from her collection of *Brenda Lee, Lesley Gore, Ricky Nelson, The Beach Boys, Connie Francis* and many more. All records proudly purchased by Mary. With her new record player blasting, her bedroom had become her own happy place.

One afternoon, Mary found one of her favorite skirts missing. She needed to find a way to lock her sisters out. She was thrilled to find a fancy key in an old chest that locked her door. Unbeknownst to Mary, it was a skeleton key that opened most doors in the house. Her sisters discovered there were more lying around. They had a field day, even though there was a *"keep out"* sign taped to the door. For Mary, this is when being a tomboy came in handy. She loved watching her dad repair things around the house. Armed with the right screwdriver, a padlock and a nasty cut on her finger, the problem was solved—or so she thought! Some of the new clothes she purchased with babysitting money continued disappearing. Frustrated, Mary said, "How is this happening, my sisters don't know the combination?" After observing more closely, she discovered the problem. The screws on the door were beginning to come loose. Mary realized the holes had gotten bigger. Her sisters were removing the paddle lock. Any time either one wanted to discover a new item to "borrow," the screwdriver became their source of bliss. Nothing was stopping them! It turned into a game, leaving Mary quite frustrated. Her sisters never gave up trying—until Mary moved out.

Mary still enjoys her drives in the direction of Walnut Hill, reminiscing about days gone by. When she stares up at the small bedroom window in the maid's quarters, Mary often wonders how she survived the heat all those summers. The house appears smaller and not as elegant. Sixty years have passed since her family lived there. Nearing 100 years old, the house is showing its age. Her late brother George's old rusty basketball hoop still hangs above the garage doors. Only a few threaded strings remain dangling after decades of use. Fond memories are all that's left, like the days of playing horse basketball with her brothers. Mary's younger sisters were closer in age, and she recalls them as being girly-girls, often playing together.

The people who purchased the home back in the 1970s continue to reside there, making few upgrades over the years. The green shades left in the 1960s still remain on most windows. The little girl named Mary who once lived there, hopes that one day Molly will gather enough courage to knock on that familiar front door…How wonderful it would be, if a request was granted to walk back in time, revisiting the maid's quarters on the third floor. Surely that would be a story for another day.

"Our feet may carry us away from home but our hearts and treasured memories remain."

Author Unknown

Forever Friends

Chapter 10

Oh those fabulous flashbacks! One thing's for certain, the longer I live, the more treasured my happier memories become. I love sitting back recalling those amusing moments in time. I'll never forget the day I met my friend Sull. It was the first day of school, when I noticed a girl from my neighborhood sitting next to me in first grade. Together we walked home becoming best friends. There was something about our personalities that clicked. Sull was bubbly and upbeat and I the more serious one. She had a way of making me laugh when no one else could. Coming from large families, we made the best of things and as kids, having fun was a priority.

Although we now live miles apart, we have a forever friendship. During visits, time seems to stand still—until we notice the clock. We love sharing hilarious childhood stories that continue captivating us, laughing ourselves silly. Being seniors, Sull and I often joke about the aging process as it continues doing its thing. Luckily neither one of us really needed name tags at our 50th class reunions. We're both grateful it's been a slow and kind transformation—so far. Thanks to social media, we have ways of checking on one other to avoid any shock. Over the years, our paths have taken us in different directions— nevertheless, our bond is secure. We continue to laugh like friends, love like sisters, and the only thing lost in between—is time. I'm forever grateful for our special connection, the memories we made, and the ones we'll continue to make.

As children of the '50s and '60s era, Sull and I both attended St. Patrick's School. Sadly, my first grade teacher kept me back while my best buddy moved ahead…What needs to be mentioned here is how book-smart my friend Sull is. Back in school, she could read a paragraph written in Latin, translating it back to English, all without skipping a beat. No matter how much I studied and prepared, reading that same paragraph brought painful brain paralysis! The only thing I can say in my defense—I was right about Latin. Ancient language should have stayed where it belonged, in prehistoric times. After all, who speaks Latin anyway? For years, even the priests have stopped saying Mass in Latin. I believe if we'd been taught Spanish, it would have served everyone better. Hindsight is wonderful isn't it?

Around the time Sull moved ahead in grade school, we slowly developed new friendships. Despite the separation, our paths crossed from time to time. We grew close again in our early teens and that's when the fun and excitement began…

Back in the day, good friends often gave each other nicknames. My best friend had hers and decided I needed one. Seeing my frustration dealing with frizzy hair in humid weather, Sull announced my forever nickname, Frizz! And yes, it was easy for her having long straight brunette hair with perfect bangs. During the "Beatles" era, it was tough trying to be "groovy and in style." After all, trendiness is the essence of self-esteem for any teen. Needless to say, when I wanted to be hip like Sull, I'd straighten my hair using my mother's iron and ironing board. I never knew the awful smell of burning hair until my first attempt at straightening! I became a contortionist trying to get all sections straight. There's no comparison to today's convenient, heat controlled, handheld flat irons, used solely for this purpose.

In summer of '63, the weather was warm, birds were singing, and love was in the air. Well the love part had to be repressed for me and Sull. Being almost 15, the boys were starting to notice us! Thank goodness our parents were overly protective and a bit on the strict side. Dating was out of the question, however, nothing was said about flirting. We needed a little boost to our self-esteem. Sull and I saw little harm in getting attention from the mature boys with cars. Back in the day when the population in our town was small, we walked everywhere and it was safe. We loved strutting through town barefoot, wearing bellbottoms, tie dye shirts and smiles. How exciting it was seeing how many honks we'd get from boys driving by. It all seemed innocent back then. Boys were rarely disrespectful and yes, we got a slew of honks!

While eating ice cream on my front porch, Sull brought up a great idea, or so we thought. She said, "Did you hear there's an agency in Boston looking for teen models? I bet we could be models but how would we get there, Frizz?" I mentioned taking a bus into the big city. Once agreed, we decided to clothes shop and possibly purchase a little make-up. Once in Mammoth Mart, we realized our babysitting money wasn't enough. We wanted to look spiffy going into Boston but we were short on cash.

With one person on the register that day, it was hectic. We whispered to one another about the money shortage, deciding to tuck the mohair sweaters we couldn't afford into our big pocketbooks. I must say we were scared silly. Neither one of us had stolen before. As we walked swiftly towards the exit, Sull walked ahead of me. That's when I noticed a sleeve hanging out of her purse. My heart was pounding out of my chest, I couldn't escape fast enough. Due to having second thoughts, we didn't know whether to laugh or cry once outside. Both of us became frightened we'd get caught with jail awaiting us! After all, my dad was a policeman. Being a bit dazed, we continued walking to the bus stop, awaiting our get away. The problem was our consciences began eating at us. Our Catholic upbringing came into play. We darted back to the store, missing the bus to return the sweaters. Without being noticed, we left them in the dressing room and hurried from the building feeling lighter and free from sin! I seem to recall rolling on the ground laughing hysterically! Surely we were overwhelmed with feelings of relief…Another lesson learned—stealing never again crossed my mind or should I say, never acted upon.

Needless to say, we found our way into Boston wearing our best apparel. It was a long and difficult day. Once all the girls lined up, we were told to walk the runway one by one. I felt like a piece of meat being inspected by several onlookers taking notes. We weren't sure how to strut our stuff so inevitably we looked clumsy. Whatever we did, it wasn't in our favor.

If memory serves me right, we were never told why we couldn't model. One of the judges had no problem telling me to stay in school. I remember having thoughts of not being tall enough. Whatever the reason, our self-esteem took a hit. Once outside, we scrambled to find the next bus home. In between teardrops, we spotted a nearby phone booth where Sull called her mother, who eagerly picked us up, consoling us all the way home. Our modeling career was over before it began… In the end, it was truly a humbling experience for two young teens.

As lifelong friends, there is one poignant memory held close to our hearts. My late brother George had taken a fancy to my friend Sull when she was "sweet sixteen." They went on several dates before he joined the Navy. Life had pulled them in different directions and both eventually found partners in marriage. They too never lost touch until

George's life was cut short at 36…We continue sharing happy memories, however, we also share the pain of George's death, creating a deeper bond between us…

A beautiful saying, *"**People come into our lives for a reason, a season, or a lifetime.**"*

My Friend Sull came into mine for all three!

Sisters, Gifts from Heaven

Chapter 11

Another Monday, and the alarm clock never went off. Mom's hollering was our back-up, making for an alarming situation—we were late for school! Martha and I dashed from the house without our boots. Trudging through puddles and thick slush left our feet wet, shriveled and cold in class. Having teenage brains allowed our looks to win over common sense. I actually thought wearing a miniskirt, nylons and new flats might have gotten us a ride from one of the high school boys. Middle school was a half mile walk for Martha while the trek for me was over a mile to the high school. Being the older more serious type left little room for conversation along the way…Out of nowhere Martha asked, "How is it that we both ended up with the smallest bedrooms in the attic?" We agreed that moving into our large three-story home allowed us choices.

I said, "Surely Mom and Dad are grateful we're in the attic and out of their hair. It certainly makes for a peaceful life for them, don't you think? Besides, we like being far away from our pesky brothers and parents, right?" Martha smirked in full agreement…Much of our spare time was spent in the finished attic with an extra door at the bottom of the stairs—a door our parents were thankful for. They no longer had to hear the uproar of three girls working out their differences. Unless of course they heard a crash or ghastly screams.

When we first moved in, I laid claim to my modest bedroom. Martha picked the smaller of the two others because of privacy issues. Otherwise, their youngest sister Sue would have to walk through the larger room to get to the other. Knowing these attic rooms were once slept in by maids made things intriguing. As young teens we'd joke with friends about living in the haunted maid's quarters. The stories we told made for many visits to the confessionals. It certainly would've been nice having maids around, if only to pick up after us. Clothes thrown everywhere, food, cups, wrappers scattered throughout, and beds left unmade. It became futile for Mom to climb three flights of stairs to clean our rooms every day. Living in cluttered spaces became a blessing and another lesson learned. Once the three of us married and moved out, we all became clean freaks. It was always the first thing people noticed when anyone dropped by my home.

Every Easter from the time we were babies, Mom loved dressing us up for church. As small children we wore matching outfits with Easter bonnets, white gloves, ankle socks and of course shiny black or white patent leather shoes. As young teens, the first thing we insisted upon was those sexy nylon stockings. How great it felt ditching the white socks and wearing shorter skirts we picked out ourselves. After Mass, Martha wanted to take pictures of us all gussied up. If it wasn't for my sister, there'd be far less photos of past events. She loved taking pictures, especially family photos.

On this particular Easter, when Martha was dressed in her pretty yellow suit, she had gotten sick. It wasn't a virus she contracted, nor was it contagious! As memory serves me, my youngest brother John had a small pet goldfish. Unbeknownst to my sister, he put his fish in a tall blue colored aluminum tumbler and left it on the bathroom sink while cleaning his fishbowl in the kitchen. Mom left these colored tumblers for rinsing after brushing our teeth. Feeling thirsty, Martha headed for the dimly lit half bath on the first floor. Seeing the tumbler filled to the brim, she began drinking it. Her eyes widened once she realized a live fish was heading down her throat! With no options and the fish disappearing, she gagged and screamed uncontrollably. Family members came running, only to discover we had different reactions to the situation. Mom responded by urging Martha to swallow a raw egg causing her to throw up. Both Martha and our little brother who lost his fish were crying incessantly while the older ones laughed hysterically. Needless to say this put a damper on our Easter hunt. The following day, Martha went off to school completely recovered, and Mom bought John another goldfish.

Time was slipping by and life events continued to happen along the way. My brother George joined the Navy and married in his second year of service. Within a few years, I also married followed by my sister Martha. We both had baby girls we adored. The odds were stacked against us marrying so young. No matter what age, difficulties can arise for any couple for various reasons. However being in our late teens, we were not fully matured. People grow and change and if it's not together, divorce is likely. I believe those who marry young, and for a lifetime, truly found their soulmates. Martha and I weren't so fortunate.

Being young mothers, my sister and I often got together over coffee. On various occasions we would bring our baby girls to visit their grandmother. Mom enjoyed seeing her granddaughters and we loved any advice given to us. At the time, we all lived within walking distance which was important for many reasons. With so much to learn, who better to teach us than our beautiful and well experienced mother.

One day I invited my mother and sister to my apartment to watch; "*The Price Is Right.*" I expressed how much fun it was watching TV in living color! Both were surprised we could afford one. Certainly my frugal parents thought of owning one but they liked their black and white because the other was too pricy. Without saying another word, we got comfy in my small living room. After serving coffee and muffins, I turned on one of the three main channels and adjusted the antenna. After making adjustments, the picture finally came in. Both my sister and mother had a strange look on their faces. Martha noticed everything on the top of the screen was blue, the middle had a mustard yellow tone and the bottom was green. She detected a corner of the screen had peeled away showing black and white underneath. They both began to chuckle after realizing my husband and I got suckered in to buying a; *"cut to size, plastic color TV, pleasing to the eye."* A cheap stick-on invention that didn't sell well—and yes, it was a joke.

Nostalgia for the most part is bittersweet. Memories often show us how things change and how much better life can be in the present. It also helps us to enjoy and reflect on those earlier carefree years. There are times when sad recollections come to mind, such as missing a loved one. These thoughts and feelings can arise on birthdays, during holidays, or merely by glancing at a picture. A memory can appear out of the blue simply by noticing your surroundings. Just the other day I passed by youngsters playing hopscotch, a game Martha and I enjoyed playing every summer as kids. Those pleasurable moments going back with her were delightful. Holding on to these memories has helped to keep Martha alive both in spirit and in my heart. If someone were to ask, "What was the hardest part of losing your sister?" my answer would be, "not being able to say goodbye and being deprived of growing old with her."

When I write about my lost loved ones, it doesn't mean I'm stuck in the past, unhappy in the present, or afraid of the future. Sometimes it's simply a peaceful place to go when I feel a need to reminisce about happier times. When sad memories begin creeping in, I find my inner strength and set about pushing away those dark clouds. For me, it's been therapeutic to write and share my stories in hopes that others who have been on similar journeys can find strength and peace.

There's an old adage that can mean different things to different people: "Yesterday is history, tomorrow is a mystery and today is a gift; that's why they call it the present." And yes, for me, I'm content living in all three!

In loving memory of my dear sister Martha, forever missed

1951 – 1973

In May of 1973, Martha lost her way—she died by Suicide.

*In honor of **National Suicide Prevention Week**, September 7-13 each year.*

*Lifeline at **1-800-273-TALK** or **Suicide Crisis Line** at **1-800-784-2433**.*

Driving Privileges
"CIRCA 1965"

Chapter 12

One of my fondest memories as a teenager was that irrepressible desire to get behind the wheel of a car. After watching how easy it was for others, I was convinced of my readiness to drive. All I had to do was put the keys in the ignition, my foot on the brake, the shifter in drive and the pedal to the metal.

Surely everyone can relate to those feelings of having butterflies in our bellies sitting in the driver's seat for the first time. I had those and then some! Although I must admit, my first experience behind the wheel brought a troublesome situation—I had my permit to drive, as long as there was a licensed adult in the car…On one particular day, there wasn't an adult around. My parents were away until evening and my brother Georgie was off to college. There, parked in the driveway, was his fancy blue 1960 Chevy with an awesome-sounding stereo. My girlfriends were relentless trying to sweet talk me into taking them for a ride. The keys were hung in the usual spot, creating temptation…No longer able to resist, I found myself up for the challenge. Having my learner's permit and staying on familiar streets should keep me out of mischief, at least that's what I thought…

After everyone piled in with me behind the wheel, the first problem presented itself. I needed to figure out the shifter in the column and the extra pedal on the floor. On rare occasions, I've watched my dad and brother drive cars with standard transmissions. I said to myself, "With the support of my friends, I can do this!" As we sat in the driveway listening to *"Help"* by the Beatles, I familiarized myself with the three gears, ready for the ride of our lives!

Backing out of the driveway should have sent neighbors running out to stop the car. Starting and stalling was unequivocally frustrating. This should have been my first indicator to park the car and leave it right where it was. But no, being stubborn and determined, I continued on. Once in third gear, it had become easier. We were beginning to enjoy the ride until I approached a steep hill with a stop sign. I tried several times to get the car on to the next street but found it kept rolling back on to someone's property. I remembered thinking, "Where are the police when you need them? I need help getting out of this embarrassing situation!" No one in the car had a permit or a license. I had to rely on myself. I distinctly remember saying, "I'll keep taking a right, that way I'll get everyone home quickly." My next attempt was successful as I turned right on a fairly level street. All went well until we neared the end and had to bear right under a railroad bridge. In front of me was another stop sign and a slight incline. Again the car stalled and I wasn't out far enough to see if there were oncoming cars. As I was about to enter a four-lane road, I thought about closing my eyes in prayer. As usual, I stalled out yet again. With fear and frustration, I started the engine, stepped on the gas, blindly ending up on the main drag.

As expected, the car stalled, only this time we were in the middle of the street...That's when I cried hysterically. This challenge had created danger not only for me but for my passengers. Someone in heaven was watching over us because there were no oncoming vehicles at the time I pulled out. There we sat, in the middle of the street, while cars went around us. The realization kicked in, I wasn't going any further. I stood outside the car and wept uncontrollably.

Peering through my blurry and swollen eyes, I noticed what looked like a convoy of army trucks coming down the road. After flagging down the first truck, we couldn't believe what we saw... When one pulled over, they all did! I remember wondering why, as this was creating way too much attention! My tears of embarrassment continued. When a soldier approached and saw a damsel in distress, he offered to drive the car home. God had answered my prayer and the ball of fire in the pit of my stomach cooled down immediately. While looking at my friends in the back seat, I noticed a healthy pinkish color returning to their once pale faces.

Just as we began to drive away safely, the convoy of trucks full of Army soldiers began following us. There must have been a dozen large trucks with an open Jeep in front. I recall asking; "Why does everyone have to follow us home?" The Army Officer explained; "We're the National Guard on a weekend mission and as a convoy, we stick together." I wasn't impressed because all I could think about was the attention this would draw in my neighborhood. Surely everyone would see these trucks and wonder if there was a war pending. Worst yet, someone would tell my parents! There was reason to be nervous although I was glad everyone was safe.

Once in the driveway, I was happy to see there had been no one home and no sightings of our neighbors outside. We were finally safe and the car was none the worse for wear. A deep sigh of relief came over me until—the nice soldier decided to drive my brother's car into the garage. He *scraped the whole right side of the newly painted Chevy, on the garage frame*—leaving evidence of shiny blue paint behind!

And yes, it was another hard lesson learned. My punishment fit the crime. It was months before I was allowed to go for my license. Nonetheless, I was prepared and certainly experienced with standard transmissions. That long-awaited morning finally came when my dad drove me to the registry. After taking the written test, the Registry Examiner took me for my driving test. After finishing the easiest part, he had me driving up the steepest hill to parallel park. During the exam, I balanced the clutch and gas pedal like I had done it all my life. I passed the test on my first try, bestowing feelings of much needed relief. Behind the wheel driving home, I was proud to be legally licensed and a privileged driver.

Me & My 1965 Beetle

Chapter 13

What a blast, driving around in my brand spanking new green Beetle! Alright, not exactly mine, nevertheless I felt differently once the keys were handed over. How did it come about having two new Volkswagens parked in the driveway? Well, from what I recall, my dad had been awarded several certificates for being the top notch salesman. They were hung like prizes in his home office. For him, making deals meant a win every time. I believe Dad's wheeling and dealing got him two VW Bugs for the price of one. I'd seen him in action many times growing up. I'll always believe, due to his outstanding sales ability, Dad could have sold a screen door to anyone building a submarine!

At least having three cars in the driveway gave me options. The VWs were parked next to my mother's new 1966 Chrysler Newport convertible. The fancy car was the only one allowed in the garage. It didn't take long to finagle the keys to Mom's convertible. There was no question which car a teenage girl would want to be seen in. Coming from a small town on a Friday night meant driving back and forth for hours sometimes on the same street. It was a thrill driving around on a warm summer night with the top down. The memories continue to be a delight.

There was little fighting amongst the siblings over who could drive the cars. With four teenagers in our house, George and I were the only two with driver's licenses. He had gotten married the following year and the red Beetle was a wedding gift from my parents. When George's military leave came to an end, he and his wife headed back to Virginia in their shiny new bug.

Feeling a sense of newfound freedom, I was determined to find ways of driving the slick green bug more often. First, let me tell you a bit about the Beetle I became so fond of. Obviously safety wasn't a priority back in 1965. No seatbelts, airbags or other safeguarded features that I can remember. Worst yet, with no engine in front, it left little protection in a front end collision. Actually, front, rear or sides! Back then there were far fewer accidents—a reason why auto safety wasn't a big consideration… Being a teen, the only thing that mattered was blasting the hit songs with the windows down. Happy and relieved my dad took the package deal which included radios. Unlike today, having a radio back then was an option with added cost.

I must admit, I found it strange to find the engine in the back with little room in the front trunk or back seat. Nevertheless, I actually enjoyed driving a standard again.

74

It was nice to feel the road allowing more control. This particular stick shift was easy to maneuver. There was a rather odd feature when first discovering the parking brake between the two front seats. A peculiar-looking rubber thing with two *balls* separated on either side of the stick handle. Believe me, there were many jokes made about that design! Oh, and one more noticeable feature during the bitter cold season—no matter how much I blasted the heat, being warm wasn't possible!

Back in high school, kids with cars had certain hangouts. One was a nearby donut shop and the other was McDonald's where burger and fries were 15 cents. Whenever I was permitted to drive the Beetle to school, friends would pile in, squeezing as many in as possible. We'd laugh ourselves silly, packed in like sardines. It felt incredible driving around acting like a grown-up. Having a car meant freedom to hang out with friends bringing fun and excitement.

One particular evening, a few kids were planning a drag race in an empty car lot behind the donut shop. My girlfriend and I tried entering the all-male race. It wasn't long before the guys were snickering. They knew VW Beetles were famous for being slow, although the engines were quite loud when revved up. Everyone began making bets and of course I chimed in saying, "Can I make a bet on being the first car off the line?" The guys agreed while smirking once again. I'm sure they thought I was a dumb brunette. Thing is, they weren't laughing when the lightweight green bug won, at least for the first hundred feet. And yes, I WAS left in the dust!

After dinner on a Friday night, I decided to show off my driving skills in front of the boys at the donut shop. I hadn't the good judgement to realize cement curbs were there for a reason…While backing up impetuously, I hit the curb hard, pushing in both exhausts. My body became rigid with fearful thoughts, knowing the consequences I would soon face. Nevertheless, I managed to laugh with friends as if having two personalities. When I started the car, the noise coming from the exhaust was deafening. The ride home became unbearable...Mostly due to those turbulent thoughts of facing my dad on arrival.

This lesson remained with me for life due to another tough punishment. Not only could I not drive for a month, I had to turn over my small weekly pay check until the repair bill was paid in full. Also, due to his loss of faith in me, dad said, "Once you get car privileges back, I'll be watching the mileage, so you had best stay in town!" This rule was a tough one. Once I was back behind the wheel, my desire to drive without restriction, overpowered any common sense yet again! My Beetle was the only means of seeing a certain friend who moved out of town.

Therefore, one early evening when I was filling up, a young gentleman at the gas station listened to my story of woe. Being an experienced mechanic, he promised to solve my problem. He said, "Right under the hood there's a cable that allows anyone to easily disconnect the mileage." Once he finished showing me how to do it, I jumped back in and sped off. As usual, I was singing along with the hip hop music blaring out the windows. If memory serves me, I believe the shy mechanic was looking for a way to ask me out…After driving home from my friend's house and seeing my dad home, I remembered to reconnect the cable. That did resolve the constraints my father put on me, making everyone happy. The good news is I never got caught. Years later I told the story to a friend who said, "when the mechanic did that, he broke the seal, devaluing the car." Even though the green "VW Bug" was eventually traded in, thankfully—and for once in my young life— there was no backlash.

Just the same, guilt lingered with me for some time. My Catholic upbringing kept me on the straight and narrow as a rule. However, there has always been a rebellious side to me, which reared its ugly head now and then…As I reminisce those years, I can honestly say how grateful I am for my strict upbringing. Many events throughout my young life certainly helped to shape who I am today. These many hard lessons contributed to building inner strength, aiding me through the many adversities I continue to face in my lifetime.

"The more risks you allow your children to make, the better they learn to look after themselves."

Roald Dahl

Those Exciting Teen Years

Chapter 14

The mid-1960s began a time of taking responsibility in my high school years. Having my first real job at a local supermarket had given me a weekly paycheck, along with a sense of freedom. With lots of experience making errors as a newbie, lessons were learned while memories were made…After months on the job, a lightbulb went off in my head. "This would never become my lifelong career." Nevertheless, I enjoyed working with people and it definitely advanced my social life.

As I reflect on my time at the Co-op supermarket, many emotions come into play—some evoke both nerve-racking experiences along with funny situations. As a cashier, the first thing that came to mind was those antiquated registers used back then. The heavy machines added and totaled purchases only. The rest was up to the cashier's ability to know math. Clearly there is little comparison to the compact electronic registers of today, making life simple and easier for the worker.

2018…

Waiting in line at the grocery store has always been a problem for me.., patience never being my virtue. In order to escape the long lines, I'd choose between leaving the carriage of groceries, or summon up thoughts taking me back in time. Just recently, there were a few people ahead of me, allowing old memories to take hold. I noticed a young girl being trained behind the register, reminding me of my own training for the same position. Like her, my first day on the job was spent observing an experienced lady. I can still picture my trainer, swiftly and effortlessly sending items down the belt, stroking the register keys as if playing piano. I remembered thinking, "this job is definably hassle-free!" On my second day, my stern-looking boss handed me a tray of money to count, allowing me to work the register alone on a busy day. Although slow and nervous at first, things went great—at least until I noticed items marked, "3 for .89" or "5 for .99." Some customers purchased one or two of the items ignoring the special pricing. No one told me about this. That's when my anxiety hit an all-time high! My arithmetic skills would now be exposed. It's not that I didn't pass my math exams in school. Sometimes I needed to use my fingers to add. Being a teenager, I didn't want to appear stupid. Furthermore, when anxious, it was nearly impossible to work numbers in my head. Until I got the hang of it, this affected my ability to do my job efficiently.

I knew math was my least favorite subject, mostly due to my well-known brain freeze that often broke my concentration. Maybe what I had was Attention Deficit Disorder, although that was unheard of back then… Anyway, going back 50-plus years can alter or leave out a part of our memory. Funny thing is, I don't recall anyone returning with receipts or questioning my mathematical skills. Yet I remember chatting up a storm with customers in order to speed up the belt, giving a can or two away. The distraction worked well during those early training days, and meanwhile the store most likely lost inventory. It was affirmed later that other young trainees had similar ordeals.

If memory serves me correctly, a few employees were ripping things off in the store. One particular stock boy named Tim was in charge of stocking cigarettes. Back then smokes were cheap, cool and legal. "Cancer sticks" were not known to be bad for your health. Many movies and TV ads made smoking appear glamourous…Tim was sometimes seen after school selling cartons out of his trunk. In those days, sophisticated security systems didn't exist, making it easy for people to shoplift. Today, new technologies deter this type of behavior. There are electronic cameras and sensors everywhere, allowing evidence against anyone who steals. The only security devices I remember were those big round mirrors placed high in corners. It helped managers catch a shoplifter, as long as they had good eyesight and strong legs, in case of a pursuit.

2018…

Shopping early mornings always works best for me. With fewer people, it allows my stress levels to remain low. When crowded, people seem oblivious to how they maneuver or leave their carriages…Some steer them in the left lane as if living in England! I like early mornings with little distraction and less people. It affords me an occasional trip back, thinking of those Co-op days 50-plus years ago. I often find myself taking in the various scents, passing through the different departments. The meat section was where I seem to conjure up most memories. With my carriage to lean on, I'd watch the gentleman cutting, wrapping and pricing meat, still wearing the same white coats and aprons worn over a half a century ago.

1965...

After months of mastering the register and my math skills, I made the move to work in the meat department. The only woman working there quit. Of course I was thrilled because there would be no more direct dealings with customers. My youthful innocence and lack of experience allowed me to dive in, trading one set of problems for another. As a teenage girl, being in the meat room was an education in itself. It was tough being the only female in a predominantly male occupation. And yes, I worked in a large cold room with several men, all over 25 years old.

My first observation on the job was seeing the meat cutter's aprons and sleeves smeared and spotted with blood stains. Took some getting used to! Understandably, fresh sawdust was sprinkled daily on the floor. My job consisted of wrapping meat in containers, pricing each by weight and readying the packages for the display case...

Being the new girl, I was tested to see what the "gentlemen" could get away with. It was then that I felt gratitude for the nine years of Catholic school. The strict discipline and hard knocks had toughened me up, making my working there tolerable. The repulsive jokes between the men were tough to ignore. Most pertained to the type of job they did along with a few off color jokes about disagreeable customers. Of course sausage jokes were the *"wurst!"* I recall the day the guys were pushing the ingredients through the machine into the skin casing. If I got caught looking over, one of them would wink at the other and snicker. Inevitably one of the meat cutters would chuckle and say, "How many inches should a sausage be?" One day I finally retorted, *"What do you call a man with half a brain?"* I then said, *"Gifted!"* Here's another boys, *"What did God say after creating man?"* While smirking I said, *"I can do better!"* The meat room went silent and it was the last time I needed to hit back…I learned quickly what needed to be done. Survival for a young lady working in the meat department meant, standing up to the men or remain silent. After all, "ignorance is bliss."

As much as I disliked going to work some days, there was a certain stock boy who caught my eye. A handsome young man who made me laugh, causing my heart to beat faster, awakening everything inside…

1965-66

Ah, first love—that special someone who steals your heart away—the one where retrieving flashbacks comes easy. For me, falling in love for the first time was both exciting and terrifying. There was no doubt, feelings were mutual—cupid had struck hard. John was a handsome Italian with dark brown hair sleeked back in the style appropriate for the 60s. John and I dated on Friday nights after working at the supermarket. I must say, being together brought intense excitement and romance. That summer, before John left for the Navy, we'd often drive to the ocean in his Chevy Corvair with its shiny red stripe. On those delightful sultry days, we'd skip school and head for the ocean. Dodging the truant officer wasn't easy, however we were never caught. What can I say? We were two people in the throes of love, young and innocent.

Due to the draft during war time, our love affair was cut short. John had joined the service, a first real heartbreak for me. I remember the tears, feeling as though I would never see him again. I recall hearing planes flying overhead as I lay crying on my bed. Sadly our relationship could not sustain the separation, we were too young. The Viet Nam war separated many young couples, ending many romances. John and I had a whirlwind romance that never stood a chance. We wrote letters for a while, however, over time, I'm sure my immaturity gave way to a false sense that he somehow had deserted me. Over time, life separated us and we both moved on.

I love random memories that make me smile, I'll always be grateful for life's experiences. As I've matured with age, so has my love for others. In time I was able to find the kind of love that deeply bonds two people together. It's a relationship filled with dedication and support, getting us through life, for better or for worse.

1965…

Darkness Everywhere

One of the most frightening times working at the Co-op was when the lights went out around 5:15 pm. My shift didn't end until 9 o'clock that evening and I hadn't finished wrapping the remaining steaks. We were all told the store would have to close. After stepping outside, the whole town was in darkness. It felt as though the world had stood still. Everyone sensed an eerie feeling and all kinds of scary stories were circulating around. I never knew the feeling of impending doom until that evening. Surely I wasn't the only one fearing the unknown. In the 1960s, there were fears of UFOs and it appeared to be the talk of the town. Ironically, if the blackout happened today, our impressionable fears would lead us to thoughts of terrorism.

It wasn't long before my dad, who was a policeman at the time, received some information. The Northeast Coast had a power failure. It was reported to be the biggest power failure in U.S. history. It had occurred in New York State, portions of seven surrounding states including Massachusetts and parts of Canada. Over 30 million people plunged into darkness. There were people stuck in elevators, millions of commuters trapped in subways, trains

84

and office buildings. The blackout was caused by the tripping of a 230-kilovolt transmission line in Canada around 5:15 p.m., which caused other heavily loaded lines to fail, precipitating a surge of power. This all created a "cascading" affect throughout the Northeast. Luckily, everyone had their electricity restored by morning…When life throws us a curveball we take notice, appreciating all that we have. Once the family awoke the next day, normalcy returned. Everyone enjoyed their bacon and eggs, with much-needed coffee. Doors had opened for school and everything was operating as usual. I realized it was my afternoon to work at the supermarket. All day, stories of the aliens causing the blackout continued, in spite of the front page news.

In retrospect, my first job allowed growth, a chance for self discovery and love. There will always be reminders of those who touched my life in many ways. As long as there's breath in me, I'll enjoy my stroll back in time. Not to make changes, but to feel things once again. I'll forever love running into those I knew and those I've loved and lost.

It takes courage to grow up and become who we really are.

E.E. Cummings

Love or Infatuation

Chapter 15

We all know great love stories begin with attraction followed by intense emotions. With that being said, not everyone who feels heart-stirring passion for another falls in love. Sometimes it's simply infatuation. Oftentimes it can take a lifetime of experiences before these matters of the heart can be sorted out. Clearly we can all relate to that awesome feeling of being hit by cupid's arrow for the very first time. For me I was convinced it was love. Being a maturing 13-year-old, I had fallen head over heels madly in love with the ice cream man. The only thing for certain, it had nothing to do with the ice cream.

I can still visualize the white box truck with *Uncle Sam* written on the side next to his picture. That famous gentleman dressed in red, white and blue stripes, wearing a tall hat. There on top of the truck sat a hideous looking horn, always playing the same repetitive music. Unquestionably annoying for many in the neighborhood, yet for me, it was music to my ears!

When hearing the melody off in a distance, goosebumps suddenly appeared. It was the most exciting time of day, seeing *Uncle Sam* coming around the corner! Each afternoon, a blissful feeling flowed through me like an adrenalin rush. When the truck came to a stop, I'd feel my cheeks getting flushed and my heart racing every time. No matter how many attempts, I could never wipe that silly grin off my face. If he missed a day, my heart would feel as though it were aching. Something about the ice cream man all dressed in white, made my heart melt. For the longest time, I didn't know his first name. All the children called him, *Uncle Sam* the ice cream man.

In order to keep my raw feelings concealed, there was always money in my pocket from the loose change my dad would leave on his bureau. I rarely wanted ice cream with all those butterflies whirling around in my stomach each time I saw him. Thing was, *Uncle Sam* was now beginning to notice. The gentleman my heart ached for began to discern my infatuation. Clearly he was uncertain how he would handle this.

Toward the end of a drizzly summer day, there were no children to be found playing outside. Off in the distance the music could be heard, signaling the white truck would soon appear. There I was, standing alone on the corner, patiently waiting as always. Once *Uncle Sam* realized it was me, he slowed down. As he pulled up, he shut off the music and asked if I wanted an ice cream. I remember feeling nervous that day but decided on an orange Creamsicle.

With a warm smile on his face, he formally introduced himself, giving me his full name. Bob had me step inside leaving the door open. He sat behind the wheel appearing to be in deep thought. As Bob turned and caught my eye, he asked for my full name before saying; "Molly, you are a beautiful young girl, full of spirit and innocence. Being a gentleman, I must tell you to be careful when it comes to trusting older men. You may never know their intentions no matter how nice they are."— OMG, a crushing blow!!! I froze unable to get any words out. All my body wanted to do was run. My Creamsicle began melting, dripping down my shirt as tears welled up. I tried desperately to hold them back by clearing my throat. I turned to say, "thank you," and raced home. At the time, I didn't know it was humiliation and rejection I was feeling.

Looking back, it wasn't love that I felt for the driver of *Uncle Sam's* truck—it was a young girl's infatuation. Yes, he put me in my place but did this in the kindest way possible. I'll forever be grateful that my first crush was on, "*Uncle Sam* the ice cream man." Being that he was 25, my story may have had a different ending—possibly another one of those sad statistics.

It wasn't long before gray skies fell upon us as summer came to an end. Winter was fast approaching with an early display of sparkling snowflakes occupying my senses. The distraction of being back in school with friends closed the door to summer romance. Of course being young allowed quick recovery from my first serious crush. Surely cupid learned to keep a distance from me, at least for some time to come. Looking back, I recall that summer experience being a bit too painful for a 13-year-old. If someone asked me Uncle Sam's name 60 years later, I'd say it's etched in my mind like a tattoo. Admittedly, it remains an unforgettable memory that gets sweeter with time.

Another remembrance of cupid getting too close was in Catholic elementary school. A polite eighth grade boy, who wore his hair like Elvis Presley, loved walking me home from school. Together we went through some rough times with the nuns. The biggest problem was our show of independence along with having a rebellious nature. Although I had never acted out, Tim did find trouble at times. We were good friends, although I felt he had a crush on me. He was a wonderful listener who seemed to know whenever I was unhappy. Tim always found ways to make me laugh. I had no physical attraction to him, but loved hanging out with Tim and my brother George. He often stopped by our house to play his guitar. Once in high school, we began losing touch. Between working, dating and sports, we drifted apart as many childhood friends do.

As the years passed by, Tim moved away while I remained in my hometown. We rarely had contact except for one Catholic School reunion and our 25th high School class reunion. We both married others and experienced the pains of divorce. He was a private investigator and a part-time singer/songwriter. Like most creative artists, his wonderful songs and talent never made it to the top.

After a morning of raking leaves on a brisk fall day, there was a knock on my door. To my surprise, my old friend Tim who I hadn't seen for years was standing in the doorway. He dropped by for a visit and to give me a CD from a recent album he had put together. Tim had not mentioned one of his songs was dedicated to me. As we sat sipping coffee, I began paying close attention to one particular song. Tears filled my eyes in complete surprise. He reached for my hand and said; "I was devastated and heartbroken when I saw the news that George had been killed in the line of duty." As we continued listening to the CD, Tim also said; "I watched the headline news for weeks. It was shown all over the country with President Bush honoring George with the White House flag at half-staff. I was so broken by this, I wanted to find a way to support you. The decision was made to write a song the night I saw your family standing on the State House steps. It pained me to see the dark despair etched on your face, Molly. Especially when cameras captured your eyes tearing up as your dad spoke in detail, about the brutal murder of his son, your brother." Tim also said, "It was that night when the words came to me. I sat down to write and record; *"Time Runs Out."*

Before leaving, Tim and I hugged as if knowing it would be the last time we'd see each other. After closing the door, I went back to listen to the song a second time. As I began listening to the words closely, I realized he had also expressed his childhood love for me...

Tim passed away in his 50s from a heart attack. The day he knocked on my door was his last visit.

The Many Forms of Love

There are different kinds of love that can be shown in many ways. Love for family, lifelong friends, and our partners. What some of us call 'soulmate' continues to resonate in many love stories. I was 18, graduating from high school, when I met a quiet man, tall, dark and handsome. Although I wasn't looking, cupid struck once again. This time, I was ready for the arrow. It was the late 1960s, during unsettling times. Young men were still being drafted due to the Viet Nam war. Lloyd was colorblind, unable to join the service. We married right out of high school which didn't give us the necessary tools to survive marriage. We did our best during the decade we were married. The one blessing from our union was our beautiful daughter, Laura, born in 1968. Her dad was a hard worker who suffered from depression. Our marriage didn't fail because of his health issues. It was the '60s freedom era and we had differences in morals and values. Love and marriage has to be built on trust. We were unable to survive due to the missing foundational principles.

When things don't work out for whatever reason, there is often a sentiment that it wasn't meant to be. I don't believe it's that cut and dry. When a relationship ends and we move through the grieving process, most people find love once again. Still, there is something to be said about first love, that euphoric feeling making us most vulnerable. Like the sensation you get on your first rollercoaster ride, never wanting it to end. It comes around once in a lifetime, changing us forever. If we've been lucky to be in love more than once, these blissful memories are worth tapping into.

Some people have the good fortune of finding their soulmate once—lasting a lifetime. For others, it may take many times over. Most often it's better or delightfully different the second time around! Proof has been in my second marriage to Bill of more than 25 years!

~~~ Written in memory of my friend Tim ~~~

Much More Than a Hairstylist

Chapter 16

Standing behind the styling chair has been a lifelong adventure with a variety of happenings to share. Through experience, hairstylists learn that the best clients are those who are referred. Being a confident sales person is also helpful. When it comes to clients, there's an array of personalities...The client *no one can please*—the *never on time* and those who say, "*I forgot my wallet.*" I'm most grateful for those clients of few words—always happy with the results. Without them, my sanity might have been in question more than once.

My talent began presenting itself around 12 years of age. I decided to be my own guinea pig. One hot sizzler of a day, I decided to cut my bangs for the first time. I was tired of those plastic hairbands that dug into my head, keeping the curly hair out of my face. With scissors in hand, and wet hair combed forward, I began cutting just above my eyebrows. It wasn't long before a panicky feeling came over me. My new bangs began waving and shrinking as they dried. In desperation and knowing there was school the next morning, I applied Dippity-Do and scotch tape. In doing so, I stretched and straightened my bangs. Otherwise friends would have mistaken me for the Dutch Boy on the paint can. And yes, with no training, the bangs dried crooked.

It wasn't long before my confidence returned. I embarked on an experiment using my sister Martha, who volunteered willingly. I began cutting layers in her hair using mom's sewing shears. Unbeknownst to me, school pictures were being taken that week. Of course once I handed Martha a hand held mirror, she began to wail. The next day, Mom brought Martha to her hairstylist, who blended the long and short layers as best she could. The hairdresser admitted she'd seen worse.

The one important person who had faith in my creativity was my grandmother. I can still remember being 13 years old when I gave her a home permanent. Even though my confidence level was at a low point, I knew how important it was to her. I also knew if her hair came out frizzy, she'd still tell me it was beautiful…Before starting, we carefully read the directions on the over the counter box perm. Once completed, I could actually see the perm had worked, the curls snapped back and wow, what an awesome feeling… Best of all, she praised me for the wonderful haircut and having the best perm ever!

As time marched on, I found myself coloring my friends' and neighbors' hair. By the time I was 15, I'd occasionally color my own with babysitting money. Wanting to be a shade darker, the color used gave me red highlights. Because of the many compliments, I continued using the same color for several years. My dark auburn hair and blue eyes were what attracted my first husband. When I grew tired of using color and my hair grew out, he was a bit disappointed to find my natural hair color was ash brown. He thought he married a redhead.

Once in cosmetology school, I began experimenting with Mother's hair. She was delighted being the guinea pig most of the time. Unfortunately an incident occurred when her hair turned a burnt orange color. I learned quickly how to tone it down before church the next day…As time went on, I benefited from the training as well as the challenges. My confidence improved as I welcomed the hands-on experience. To my delight, I won an Award for *Best Fantasy Hairstylist*, taking first place. I weaved a hairpiece into short hair, creating a Christmas tree affect, sprayed with silver and decorated with tiny bulbs. I've kept the picture and article from the newspaper from 1970. During the course, not only did I learn colors, perms, cutting techniques and styling, I learned how to master facials, make-up, manicures and pedicures. I graduated with a license to work in all areas of cosmetology. During theory, I remember a funny story studying certain words in Latin. The class needed to know each muscle of the face. Thanks to my Catholic school background, I had some understanding of the Latin terms for the upcoming exams. The words forever planted in my brain since cosmetology school, "musculus orbicularis oris"—*translation*; "the kissing muscle." Strange how certain words stick...

Once I received my degree and was in the work force, it became a whole different playing field working with paying customers. A cosmetologist deals with the public, in some ways similar to a bartender. The job entails working with clients with different personalities and different backgrounds. Some clients are harder to please than others.

My first job started out as a shampoo girl in an upscale salon. Back in the 60s and 70s, women were 95% of a salon's clientele. A time period of big hair similar to the "Mary Tyler Moore flip" and the old fashioned "bee hive French twist."

I'll never forget my first dreadful experience. I was fresh out of school, ready to take on the world. While working as a shampoo girl the first few months on the job, the owner, also a hairstylist, went home sick. The shop was super busy and they needed me to take one of her clients. Every stylist knew this woman to be the fussiest client ever! Being in unchartered waters, I agreed to take on the challenge. I attempted my version of the late Mary Tyler Moore's hairdo, which the client agreed to. When I removed the large rollers from her hair, trouble began. I noticed the more I combed it, the more the flip began to flop. I was horrified seeing her angry face staring back at me in the mirror. My face became hot as it turned a beet red. I'll never forget the embarrassment of her jumping up from the chair and yelling, "I need help here, I'm paying for a hairdresser not a shampoo girl!"

It didn't take much for someone to straighten it out rather quickly, showing the difference between an experienced hairstylist and someone right out of school. Knowing it was another learning experience, I was determined to find the resolution. It was all about using too little product and the wrong size roller on fine textured hair. I recall a moment when I wanting to give up on my new career. However, I was resolute on not quitting because of one unhappy woman.

Unfortunately, I've known newly licensed stylists who've walked away over one bad experience, leaving scissors behind. It's difficult being a new beautician in the learning phase. A career can end before it's begun. Often times due to an inconsiderate client.

In my late 20s I decided to open a salon in my house. I wanted to be home with my daughter during those crucial years. After acquiring my license from the town, I had become the proud owner of a professional beauty salon. Owning my own business was not only a lucrative career, I was able to work my own hours. The driving force for making it happen sooner rather than later was because I was being sexually harassed by my boss. I learned over the years he had harassed many of the girls who worked for him. Today he would have paid a big price. Woman didn't report these things back then.

If I had the ability to make a change in the cosmetology program, I would add a psychology course as part of the school curriculum. I've found over the years that clients often view us as their therapists. Many share deep and personal problems with their stylists. For instance, I remember one unforgettable situation in my salon. As I was cutting a woman's hair, she began to cry. After I sat and held her hand, she started to talk about the loss of her daughter to ovarian cancer. This pain on her face brought tears to my eyes.

Over time, I've learned the importance of listening. Especially when someone is going through something we don't always understand. I've also found it's about having patience, while showing the client both empathy and grace on a personal level. There have been many situations over the years that have taught me lessons. During those 45-plus years, I can honestly say, being a hairstylist is so much more...

Giving Back

Chapter 17

Waking up in a swanky hotel suite on my honeymoon was supposed to be one of the happiest days of my life. In every sense of the word it truly was. In our hearts both Bill and I knew we had it right this time around. He's the love of my life and, as time passes, I'm certain feelings are mutual. With time and patience, we successfully blended our families. It's been an earnest commitment to spend the rest of our lives together, for better or for worse. We were both born in 1949 and although Bill is one week older, we married at 42 years young! The evening we got engaged, Bill had one request—to marry on his birthday. What was his rationale? He never wanted to forget our anniversary. Of course as the years go by, I've understood the method to his madness. You see, on more than one occasion, it was I who forgot our wedding anniversary. We married on Friday the 13th and I'm quite sure there was an Irish curse connected to that date. Love being blind, I took the plunge in spite of a possible scourge placed upon us. Surly my Irish mom has turned over in her grave, at least once. Hopelessly optimistic, I tend to love Fridays, even though our wedding day landed on doomsday.

When I awoke that morning, the sun was beaming through the windows. We had a fabulous day planned out. As I began getting ready, a familiar and scary feeling came over me. I felt that same ache in my lower pelvis that I felt as a child. Once in the shower, I decided to brush it off to the honeymoon activities. Our plan was touring the art shops in Rockport and spending a romantic dinner by the ocean. I felt by drinking more water and finishing the day relaxing together, I'd feel better and the discomfort would resolve itself.

It was a balmy day with plenty of sunshine. We did a lot of walking, causing frequent stops in places with restrooms. Due to my fatigue, we decided to skip the beach and head back to the hotel. That night was the most difficult time. The pain increased and I couldn't wait to head home to see my doctor for what I thought was a urinary tract infection, something I have not had to deal with since childhood. The dark and scariest of memories came rushing back.

Once home, I was immediately seen by my doctor and antibiotics were started. The physician tried several different kinds to no avail. I then started my lengthy search for doctors who all gave the same answer: "there was no infection." The pain became a daily problem and it was frightening not knowing what was happening. I wasn't going to live my life with this chronic pain. Being both relentless and proactive, there'd be no giving up or giving in. When no one gave me answers, I went into research mode, determined to find an answer. Having a computer in the home was not the norm back in the early 1980s. Most of my research had to be done at the library. Finally after several hours, I came across a large book that explained women's health issues in detail. There in one small paragraph on page 463, was the symptoms I was experiencing... Bringing this information to my urologist, he did a cystoscopy and the diagnosis was made. It was the condition I feared. Interstitial Cystitis had no cure and no optimal treatment. I knew this to be a debilitating condition as it was affecting every part of my life.

Over time and after continued research, I decided to approach this new challenge in my life conservatively. It took educating myself and going through many months of trial and error. For me, certain foods, vitamins and medications with certain inert ingredients caused my flare-ups. I joined a small group educating myself on many levels. I also began to notice certain patients weren't responding as well as I had. There were many reasons for that—what works for one patient doesn't always work for another. No matter what illness we face, it's imperative to be our own best advocate.

There was a time period when I barely left home except when things were needed. Most days were difficult, nevertheless, there was light at the end of the tunnel. As I began to have better days, I offered a promise between myself and God. I asked for strength and healing so that I could give back by advocating and supporting other IC sufferers. My prayers were answered...At the time there were no support groups on the East Coast. I reached out to other IC sufferers and started a group in 2000, watching it grow to be one of the largest in the country. *The Boston*

Metrowest IC Support Group welcomed hundreds of IC patients over my 10 years as leader and founder. With the help and support of the ICNetwork and the Interstitial Cystitis Association, they provided information and posted my meetings on their websites. Many patients came from far and wide. Some came only until their symptoms became manageable, while others were regulars and enjoyed making friends. I have always proclaimed the importance of supporting one another due to the difficulties IC presents in a patient's life.

For me, the hardest part of being a leader was the inability to help those few patients who couldn't find relief. Most patients were able to get their symptoms under control. A small few had unrelenting pain and/or frequency no matter what treatment they tried. One particular gentleman had experienced severe symptoms and with my recommendation and a prescription from his doctor, he found relief although it was short lived. I spent hours talking with him only to hear frustration and pain in his voice. Dennis was a well-respected, prominent businessman in his home town. He had a very active lifestyle with his wife and three boys until IC took over. Jogging and bicycling were his favorite ways to unwind, until they became things that he no longer could do. One day in late spring, I received another call from Dennis, again searching for answers to help the unrelenting pain. He was becoming desperate because not only did the medication stop working, he also felt he had exhausted everything. We talked again for some time, supporting him as much as possible. Listening was all I could do…I couldn't fix what was happening to Dennis.

It was early fall and I had been preparing for another large IC forum in October. While doing my usual mass emailing, something strange had happened. A "failed return" email came back from Dennis's business. I not only found this odd, I had a terrible gut feeling deep inside. I realized I hadn't spoken with Dennis over the summer. My keen sense of concern and a bit of courage allowed me to reach out and call his work place. The secretary answered and after introducing myself, I asked to speak with Dennis, however, she hesitated… My concerning words must have been heard because she opened up by saying, "Molly, he was killed in a crash." She explained that he left for lunch one day and never returned. The Police found his vehicle with Dennis inside. He smashed his new SUV into a tree, bursting in flames. After the police examined the scene, they had estimated he was going well over 100 miles an hour, aiming directly at a tree in the woods. There were no brake markings. Sadly my gut feeling was right. I was far too familiar with the cause of most suicides. The picture in the newspaper of his smoky burnt SUV with the image of Dennis inside will remain in my mind forever. He was a handsome man, in the prime of his life. The unrelenting pain had taken over, causing complete loss of hope.

During this time period I'd been doing research on suicide and Dr. Jack Kevorkian. Although he has passed since, most everyone knew him as the euthanasia proponent who assisted terminal patients' right to die. I had discovered during my research that two of his assisted suicides were IC patients. However, IC is NOT a terminal illness. The realization had set in as to how serious this disease could be even through my own past experiences. Within the 10-year period of being a leader, I had known three IC sufferers in my group who ended their lives… On a more positive note, there is a high percentage of patients who find treatments, living full and happy lives.

In my tenth year as support group leader, another distressed gentleman came to our meeting for the first and only time. He was in so much pain he couldn't sit or stay. Seeing the pain and desperation, I reached out to him with individual support and information. I also asked if he could join us for our next meeting. Others were approaching me with questions and when I turned around, he was gone. I wasn't able to get his full name but had hoped to see him at our next meeting. Several meetings took place and he hadn't returned. Months passed by, and he often came to mind as I prayed he had found a different answer than Dennis. He appeared distraught that day…Later that year we had our annual October Forum with guest speakers. While chatting with patients, out of the corner of my eye appeared the gentleman I remembered. Once he recognized me, he maneuvered his way through the crowd. He touched my arm gently while quietly saying, "I can't stay because there's family waiting in the car. I made this trip to personally thank you for saving my life that day." My heart was deeply touched! After the day was over, feelings of inner peace washed over me. My promise to God had been fulfilled. That day revealed the importance of helping others. Although I had to retire, I continue taking phone calls from IC patients. Often times all a sufferer needs is someone to listen…

In memory of all my IC friends who lost the battle.

Dennis

Deb

Doris

Awake and Watching

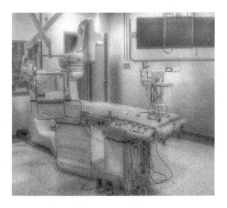

Chapter 18

L ife can sometimes be scary and out of control. As
humans, we love and desire excitement! In return
for this adrenaline rush we seek, our heartrate
increases to compensate. This sensation sometimes feels as
though our hearts are pounding or rapidly racing. Luckily,
most of us are unaware of these internal changes. Once the
exhilaration is over, with a few deep breaths and a short
passage of time, our heart rate begins to slow in response to
the mind and body calming down. We all know this is the
natural "fight or flight" response, when our body is in good
health and everything is in sync. When our internal body
system is working correctly it's taken for granted—until we
are made aware something's not quite right.

Recently, according to the news media, a Rookie blue liner for the Boston Bruins, *Charlie McAvoy* had a catheter ablation procedure, giving him his life back. Like me, he had a condition called super ventricular tachycardia (SVT). He was diagnosed at 20 years young. SVT can be diagnosed at any age and it's not uncommon. It's been said by the medical community to be a benign condition and doesn't cause death unless there's an underlying issue. My doctor once said; "As we get older, a racing heart, that frequently paces over 140 beats for hours, can wear down over time."

After the death of my mother, I began suffering from "panic attacks" or rapid heartbeat. It turns out these events may well have been a result of my having SVT. I was unaware of these episodes until it became more pronounced in my 50s. It got to the point my world was becoming smaller. By the time I reached my 60s, I was enduring bimonthly ER visits because the Valsalva maneuver didn't always work. At times I was brought in by ambulance as the tachycardia was happening more frequently. Either in the ambulance or upon arrival, that awful medicine *Adenosine* would be given intravenously. Once injected, it stops the heart for seconds, often returning it to normal beats. A very strange and frightening feeling when first injected.

For many years I believed these palpitations were caused by a panic disorder. Once diagnosed, doctors continued to reassure me SVT was a "benign" condition. As mentioned, there are healthy athletes and children with this condition. It is unquestionably alarming when someone's heart rate gets up over 150 to 300 beats per minute, anywhere from 20 minutes to hours on end. When I became aware this was happening to me, it didn't seem benign, it was terrifying!!! It greatly affected my quality of life.

My condition was very sporadic. These episodes occasionally happened during emotional duress, after exertion, or during a great deal of excitement. There were times it happened for no reason, as if someone flipped a switch. I could be gazing at a beautiful sunset only to have another episode. I began connecting the dots, realizing that, in years past, I stopped doing things that raised my heart rate, probably due to SVT. It wasn't until my late 40's that these episodes happened for no apparent reason. With more frequent visits, the ER nurses knew me by my first name. I told myself it was time to do something or take a job at the hospital. Like most, I was skeptical about a procedure recommended by a cardiologist. Eventually I took a stance, letting go of the "what ifs" that were engulfing my mind.

I just knew I was sick of allowing SVT to control my life's existence. Simple things such as relaxing with friends, going on vacation or a simple road trip became a huge worry for me. Will I have another episode? What if there isn't a hospital nearby? Only another arrhythmia sufferer could possibly understand what this can do to your psyche. It controlled much of my life and I knew a decision had to be made.

After much research, I took the scary leap, making an appointment for the ablation procedure. I imagined having no more fear of another episode, especially after learning this procedure had a high success rate and my condition could be corrected. Fortunately I lived near Boston where we have the best hospitals in the country. My appointment was scheduled with a very skilled electrophysiologist, Mark E. Josephson, MD, one of the best in the country! He was the chief of the Division of Cardiovascular Medicine within the Cardiovascular Institute at Beth Israel Deaconess Medical Center as well as the Herman Dana Professor of Medicine at Harvard Medical. He was the director of the Harvard-Thorndike Electrophysiology Institute and Arrhythmia Service.

On March 23, 2014, the day of my procedure, I arrived at the hospital by 7:00 am and by 11:00 am, was in the EP lab. I had read many people were unwilling to go through this procedure without anesthesia, however, after speaking with my doctor, I reluctantly agreed to be awake! A very scary scene being wheeled in, seeing all the latest equipment and knowing I would be both the patient and observer. They hadn't given me anything to take the edge off. Dr. Josephson had mentioned that all too often if a patient is medicated or put out, the heart can go to sleep as well. This would make it harder or near impossible to find the faulty pathways.

So there I was, getting a defibrillator attached to my back in case of a heart attack. My arms and legs had been tied down with Velcro straps to keep me from moving. Talk about giving up all control, something I was not good at. Looking around at the sterile room and the EP team, I noticed they were dressed in white gear from head to toe. Similar to the suits they use to keep from contracting Ebola, minus the head gear. When I asked about their gear, one nurse said; "to keep us safe from radiation." I then thought to myself, "why wasn't I protected, all I was wearing was a gown with a thin white blanket draped over me!"

They began by numbing both sides of my groin area before inserting the flexible catheters. After watching the screen close by, I noticed one catheter had moved toward the direction of my heart. The EP specialist working with the doctor and the team paced my heart to trigger SVT by creating PAC's in increasing succession. Once in SVT, the doctor can see exactly where the pathway is via fluoroscopy, (a type of x-ray that allows motion) 3-D imaging which is produced by the use of CARTO equipment. The doctor burns that area of the heart to break the pathways.

Everything in the sterile environment was all state of the art. The team had continued working more than three hours as they raced my heart to find the misfiring of my heart's electrical system. After the procedure was over, the nurse quietly leaned over and said; "You did very well—oh and by the way, your heart just did three marathons!" "Wow, to think I didn't even break a sweat…"

My quality of life is back and I am SVT free!!! I was 64 when this procedure was done. It's been over five years and it's now safe to say, I am officially cured!

I'm forever grateful for the highly skilled work of Dr. Josephson and his team. I highly recommend anyone with a heart rhythm disorder to find the best EP cardiologist and have this procedure; it changed my life and can change yours!

In memory of Dr. Mark E. Josephson who gave me my life back.

May he Rest in Peace. A doctor truly missed!

Happiness Within

Chapter 19

Happiness can be elusive and it's many things to different people. Most of us rely on our inner sense of well-being to feel good. When everything is right in our own world, our state of mind tends to be in a happy place. Happiness can be enhanced through small pleasures such as being in love, enjoying holidays or simply watching a sunset. For some, happiness comes easy despite whatever comes their way. There are also those who seem to have everything but never achieve satisfaction. One thing we know for sure: happiness can't be bought with money. We also know happiness is largely subjective. We control our destiny by the choices we make and how we live our lives. Making the best decisions for ourselves often leaves us with feelings of well-being.

Listening to my generation of music reveals my best and worst emotions. There were love songs, such as, *'My Happiness,'* one of Elvis Presley's first recordings in 1953. In 1958 Connie Francis sang it both in Italian and English. She was my favorite. In 1965, *"Unchained Melody,"* by the Righteous Brothers was a huge hit. In 1986, Barbara Streisand had a beautiful song called, *"Evergreen."* Love songs came before me and will continue to be written and sung long after.

When it comes to families, I find one of the happiest moments is the arrival of a new member. When a baby is born, parents are elated despite the fact that their infant has yet to learn this great emotion. The first couple of months the infant relies on instinct and having immediate needs met. We know as parents we want to believe the first smile means they are responding with happiness, however, more than likely it's simply gas. Nevertheless, happiness, anger and fear eventually develop within the first year of life. When parents are consistent with love and discipline, children tend to becoming happy adults both mentally and physically.

On the morning of September 23, 1968, I awoke with terrible cramps and lower back pain. I thought, "This can't be labor, my delivery date is the second week in October." After getting up and moving around, I knew something was happening. Cell phones were unheard of back then and my first husband would be hours on the road. It seemed only minutes after talking with my mother that she was at my door. Believing I was in labor, she grabbed my suitcase, got me into her '68 Chevy Malibu and drove haphazardly through traffic. Mom flew through several yellow lights—maybe red—neither one of us had recalled much that day. Having arrived in one piece, I'd say we were carried in on angel wings.

Back in those days, husbands and family weren't allowed in the labor or delivery room. The nurse that escorted me in a wheelchair to the labor unit insisted my mother leave. Reluctantly Mother turned and walked away.

The closer we got to the labor room, the more panic-stricken I'd become. Once the automatic doors opened, several women were either screaming in pain or cursing their husbands who weren't there. I said to the nurse, "That's it, I'm not staying—I'm going home!" With a stern face she replied; "You won't get far, you can't do this without our help." Seeing little to no choice, I ended up covered with white sheets on a gurney with tall stirrups. I became more frightened seeing a large grumpy nurse standing over me with the biggest hands I'd ever seen. She could barely get a rubber glove on. This didn't stop her from using her fingers, checking to see if my cervix had dilated. I screamed as loud as I could and after that—remembered nothing!

In the 1960s, it was common practice for doctors to use twilight sleep. I was given a potent cocktail causing unconsciousness for many hours. Being so young, and in that time period, there were no other options. Since then I've done research and found it wasn't in a child's best interest to be born this way. There may have been many children negatively affected in ways not realized or able to be proved. Babies had to be delivered by forceps, including mine. Given I wasn't able to help or be a part of the birth, my insides were ripped. I had an episiotomy with 22 stitches inside! My baby was born with a cone shaped head and a swollen eye due to this type of birthing. We were told immediately it would normalize and she'd have a perfect shaped head. In a short time she was perfect! We named her Laura Lee with her beautiful rosy cheeks, green eyes and a hint of blonde hair. Her proud dad agreed as he passed out cigars. Thing was, dads were not a part of the birthing and I believe this may have caused a bit of disconnect with their new babies.

As a mother, my happiest moments were seeing the world through my daughter's eyes. Especially when Laura was a little girl, I loved feeling her joy and excitement. As a parent, I've experienced lots of intense emotions watching my child grow. My fondest memories—seeing her first smile when I kissed and blew on her tummy—watching her taking those first steps—letting go of her new bike when she first learned to ride—seeing her glow as she blew out her birthday candles. It's these rewinds we mustn't let disappear. Those are precious moments—memories in the making—the kind I'm grateful to have.

If I were to sum up happiness through my own life's experiences, it would have to be what brought me joy and contentment. These emotions are intertwined. Simplicity has played an important role when it comes to feelings of happiness. Wanting more or trying to acquire more was not what brought me contentment. Once I learned this, I didn't need more. Laughter and/or joy always came unexpectedly from life's little things. When it comes to being happy in relationships, it's about loving someone for who they are and not how we wish them to be. This has worked through my own experiences. Inner peace and contentment is strongest when helping others. Happiness will then follow…

"Happiness depends upon ourselves"

Aristotle

A New England Christmas with My Daughter

~ 1975 & 1982 ~

Chapter 20

Sitting by the toasty fire inspired me to finish addressing the last of my holiday cards. Outside, the blustery winds were creating snow drifts. The forecast of blizzard conditions was now upon us throughout the evening. These types of storms are expected in the northeast and this was a doozy. The snow was accumulating quickly, and the drifting began blocking all exits in my house. Feeling a bit anxious peering out, the windswept snow could be seen creating small tornado affects and at times blowing sideways. The cement-like snow began sticking to the windowpanes making visibility nearly impossible…It would be late morning before I entertained any thoughts of shoveling out.

After dinner, my daughter Laura and I scurried to our rooms. We changed into our flannels and slippers, anxious to hunker down for the evening. With hot chocolate in hand, we talked about the lovely morning and the drive to the farm for our freshly cut Christmas tree. Having a tight budget, we picked one missing a few branches. With a smile I said, "We have plenty of garland and lots of decorations, we could make it close to perfect!" Laura began laughing and said, "Or we could call it our Charlie

Brown tree." It was such a joy sitting with my daughter by the fireplace with its flames aglow. The mantle showcased the decorative candles with holly branches spread from one end to the other. Below, red velvet stockings hung, awaiting festive presents and treats from Santa. Once the fragrant balsam tree is decorated on Christmas Eve, our forever tradition is to place an angel on top, completing the blessings of the season.

In spite of the icy snow pelting against the windowpane, there was radiating warmth felt inside. As I sat with my daughter, life seemed to stand still for one glorious evening. The holiday hustle and bustle had been put on hold. We began talking about a neighbor who once loved celebrating Christmas but was now elderly and living alone. There was a time when Mrs. Kiley displayed colorful lights and wreaths garnishing the front of her home. Laura asked, "Mom, what happened to her? I rarely see Mrs. Kiley anymore. She's had no decorations displayed for a number of years." I replied, "Laura, do you remember her only son Joey who went into the service? You met him a few times however you were very young. Joey was killed overseas, and Mrs. Kiley never got over the loss of her only child." After a bit of silence, Laura perked up saying, "I have a great idea! Let's invite Mrs. Kiley for Christmas dinner?" I agreed whole heartedly. We continued sipping our cocoa as we reminisced Christmases of past. Looking at my daughter, I became acutely aware my beautiful 14-year-old girl was growing up.

"Laura, do you remember the year we had another big snowstorm on Christmas Eve and the lights went out?" I reminded her she was seven years young—understandably impatient and anxious that particular year… "With tears, you said, 'Mom will this much snow keep Santa away?' " Without thought I explained, "Nothing in the world would keep dear old Santa from stopping by. He'd never forget a special little girl." You seemed somewhat content with the answer and went back to reading your Christmas books… "Do you remember telling me the only gift you wanted from Santa was a goldfish?" Laura seemed puzzled at first before she spoke. "That's right.., it was one of those "life's disappointments'—a learning moment on self-pity." "Boy am I glad you said that! Let me fill you in… It was Christmas Eve, snowy and bitter cold outside. I had your goldfish well hidden in the closet. We lost our electricity for several hours that evening. Of course you were up early so I lit the fireplace to ramp up the heat before opening our gifts. There you were, my little girl under the tree, impatiently waiting to open presents. I headed for the closet to get the surprise goldfish in its beautifully decorated bowl…Once there, I couldn't believe my eyes, the fish was floating sideways. My heart sank and I had to think on my feet quickly! I recall closing my bedroom door before telling you to sort out the presents while I found something warm to wear. Sadly, behind closed doors, the goldfish got a quick burial. With a swift flush, it whirled around slowly until it disappeared out of sight. The water in the fishbowl needed to be drained carefully due to the tiny colorful stones and plants. While handing you the bowl with a big red bow attached, I insisted, Santa wanted you to pick out the prettiest goldfish as soon as the store opens. No matter what words sputtered out, you weren't happy. I couldn't say the fish froze overnight, you were too young to explain death!" Nevertheless, we were in stitches as we shared another memory.

After opening presents, we enjoyed the fresh baked blueberry muffins, shoveled, and headed off to church. While driving, Laura and I shared thoughts of the true meaning of this magical day. We didn't know the exact date of the birth of Christ or when Christians first began to celebrate Christmas. Nevertheless, it's become a celebration for many centuries. I believe it was around the thirteenth century when Christmas carols were first being heard. Like ours, most Catholic families participated in the yearly tradition of midnight Mass in the mid-1900s. It was a tradition and kids loved staying up. When the organ begins playing and the choir sings, those mystical sounds bring memories of yesteryear.

Once we arrived home, I placed the sirloin roast and baked potatoes in the oven while Laura prepared the green bean casserole. Mrs. Kiley arrived around 3 p.m., truly grateful for the company and the wonderful meal. She was comfortable talking with us about her son Joey, a brave soldier who received the Purple Heart. I could see the toll this had taken on her. The light in her eyes had grown dim and her smile, less radiant—all indications of a broken heart. "Losing a child no matter what the circumstances is an out of order death," she said. "Only those who walk this lonely path, grieving for their child, will know this pain. I count my blessings knowing each day brings me one day closer to being with my Joey, in eternity."

With another holiday coming to a close, we took a drive that evening, enjoying the last of the snow-covered decorations. Traveling along Main Street, we spotted a few Victorian houses with large icicles hanging from the roofs' edges, and snow-covered wreaths garnishing the doorways. The downtown lamp posts were wrapped in greenery with tiny lights shining through. On the common children were frolicking in the snow. The trees seemed to be touching the sky with their colored lights and decorations. These yearly traditions with all their beauty are reminders of what's important in our lives. There's nothing more magical than making memories as a family.

Snuggled in bed that evening, I began to ponder the true meaning of Christmas. As children, we tend to be self-centered, wanting "things" that make us happy. When the holidays come around each year, children expect to get everything they've wished for. As young adults, we're more aware that the "things" we dream about may not come true. Once we begin facing the trials and tribulations of life, the awakening emerges. We've begun to understand happiness is not found in "things." Nevertheless, we never give up hope that anything is possible and we can make "things" happen. We realize it's not always about us. Happiness comes to us on a deeper level, especially when helping others.

This brings me to the exchanging of gifts. Gift giving and receiving can be fun and full of surprises. Over time, I've come to believe it's not the presents we receive or the cash in the cards—it's about the gift of "YOU." It can be a reciprocal gift worth far more than money can buy. Whether it's giving time to someone in need, a shoulder for someone to cry on, or an ear for listening—these kind acts are the true meaning of Christmas. Giving is a celebration within and it's possible anywhere or anytime. Just imagine the abundance of love we'd have in the world... I can truly attest—helping others has been life's greatest reward.

Dad's Unmistakable Voice
Chapter 21

Episodic memory flashes flow easily when I think of my dad. Like those stifling summer evenings as a kid, when he'd drive us to Farm Pond for a swim after dinner. "Dad, can I please sit in front with you?" Being the 8-year-old allowed my oldest brother George, who was 11, first dibs. "Molly," Dad said firmly, "when your brother isn't with us, you're next in line to sit up front." Dad didn't understand why I detested being in the back seat, and it wasn't about fairness! Back then, rolling all the windows down was our only means of air conditioning. Problem was, occasionally my dad smoked cigars. When he'd spit out the driver's window, the spatter invariably flew in the back window, spraying my face!

What made our ride to the lake pleasurable was my dad's love for music. Listening to songs on the car radio lifted everyone's spirits. Sometimes he'd sing along with the best, sounding pretty darn good. Dad loved overpowering Elvis Presley's voice whenever he sang his favorite; "*Are You Lonesome Tonight.*" Dad's voice was rather distinctive, making it easy picking him out of a crowd. So much expression and emotion is how I remember him…Of course Dad's happier emotions could take a nose dive at any time! When punishment was due to any one of us, his voice changed dramatically! If that didn't work, he'd reach for his belt as last resort—mostly a scare tactic. When Mother was in charge and we were misbehaving, she'd utter sternly, "You'll be sorry when your father gets home!" Believe me, problems resolved quickly. In spite of those rare punishments, we were good kids. After all, we knew the alternative wasn't pleasant.

Although my dad was a gregarious man, he didn't do well being on his own. Family meant everything and he enjoyed earning money to keep us financially secure. When it came to political issues, all those who knew him— understood —if you don't agree, walking away was best. Otherwise an argument was probable. In many instances, Dad had no problem letting others know it was his way or the highway. He was a man of conviction, hard to convince otherwise. Especially after the horrific murder of his first-born son that forever changed him.

As a child, I remember my father looking quite handsome in his police uniform. The gun hanging from his belt was a bit frightening, being way bigger than my brothers' cap guns. Nevertheless, he was my protector. My siblings and I invariably looked up to him, vying for his attention. Having two careers and working out to stay healthy kept him busy. I recall his buddies from the Department calling him "Hoot." One of Dad's friends from the force explained decades later, he got that nickname due to his hooting and a-hollering!

By the time I was in school, I realized my family life was no different from others of that era. Fathers and mothers each had specific roles. Even though Dad was engrossed in work much of the time, it was important to him that family dined together. Besides being in law enforcement, dad became a very successful audiologist.

He was one of the few in Massachusetts to sell the body-style transistor hearing aids before the behind-the-ear models were invented. Due to his father's severe hearing loss, Dad was determined to help him by learning the business. After years of going house to house helping others, Dad's hearing also declined with age. With pride getting in the way, his hearing aid decorated his bureau more so than his ear. It became clear, speaking louder and leaving the room when the TV was blasting became our only option. Convincing him to lower it was not in anyone's best interest. Unfortunately he wasn't the one left frustrated by repetitive talk...In all fairness, there's something to be said about "selective hearing" and shutting out the "noise" for a while.

A Funny Christmas Tale

After the tragic losses of my three siblings, I also lost my mother, diagnosed with broken heart syndrome in 1987. This loss was most difficult for my dad. She was the glue that kept our family together. After her death, holidays became more significant to me. We were losing too many family members. One particular year, I made a point to reach out to extended family for a holiday gathering... As a surviving sibling, I knew how quickly life can change in the blink of an eye. Thankfully all family members joined in our Christmas celebration.

Days before the upcoming holiday, my husband Bill brought home a so-called; "fart machine" with a remote! My eyes rolled as I grumbled, "You're kidding me!" With conviction he said, "It's time to bring laughter back into our family. This gadget has realistic sounds and the kids will be in stitches. The adults and the younger ones will get a kick out it." After watching him place it under a cushion and pressing a button with his finger, the worst flatulating sounds bellowed out! With some hesitation, I decided not to be a "party pooper."

As family, we knew trying this on my father would probably produce the worst outcome. He liked jokes but not of this type...The evening arrived and everyone began gathering in our large family room decorated in poinsettias. The Christmas tree stood in all its beauty while the fireplace burned brightly. The children were stretched out on the floor while the adults sat in comfy chairs. Unfortunately the chair my father chose was the one the gadget was placed under. The "machine" was completely hidden by the wrap around skirt, dressing the bottom of the chair. Luckily Bill warned the younger kids ahead of time. They immediately began snickering, well aware of Grampy's unpredictability. We all knew we were treading on thin ice...The TV now blaring as my dad became completely engrossed in a Christmas show. Suddenly the sounds of the "machine" rippled through the room as the kids began laughing up a storm. At first my 82-year-old dad was oblivious to this sick joke being played. It wasn't long before that unpleasant look grew on his face. I knew Dad was perplexed as to why everyone seemed to be laughing at him. He finally turned around with a stern look and grumbled, "You kids, what's going on? Be quiet!" As soon as Grampy turned away, they buried their faces in pillows trying to muffle their laughter. A few adults left the room because they too were stifling their laugher. To save the night, I brought my dad his favorite martini with chips and dip. And yes, I shut off the machine to end the disturbance. Luckily my dad never knew the joke was on him. Not wearing his hearing aid that evening was both a gift and a blessing.

Dad's passing years

While the years carried my father into his 90s, the last were spent telling stories of days gone by. As a boy growing up on a farm in the 1920s, there were many demands placed on him. Acres of apple trees needed to be sprayed, picked and sold. Mom once said, "Many mornings before sunrise, your dad was yanked out of bed to work the orchard." In conversation with my dad one day I asked, "Was your dad too rough on you at times?" After deep thought he said, "Well, at times it felt awful and I resented him growing up. Now that I've had my whole life to look back upon, it was the discipline and hard work that made me who I am today. Everyone has a job to do in life and I'm grateful for those hard lessons. Molly, it was a healthy way to grow up. Drinking goat's milk, eating fresh eggs, garden vegetables and apples, gave me a long life."

When my father revisits his life stories, they're often narrated in graphic detail. One in particular had left a negative impact on him as a child. This story also leaves a permanent imprint on the minds of those who listen. For Dad, each time he rewinds back to that day, he's lost once more in the nightmare. We were told over the years our dad played the violin and ukulele as a kid. He didn't talk much about his friends who also played instruments.

Dad began his story by saying; "God must have been with me that day, otherwise I wouldn't be here telling this horrific story…My friends and I often practiced at our nearby shack we built on a hillside. We were making improvements due to the many leaks. One particular day my friend Joey said. "George, let's meet up with our buddies after school and oh, bring your violin. We need to practice for the upcoming recital while our buddy Patrick works on making the structure sturdier." I ran home from school and asked mother if I could go. She adamantly refused. Help was needed to load the truck with apples. Of course being a kid, I felt cheated out of being with my friends. While loading the bushels of apples, my dad and I heard a loud explosion coming from the direction of the shack. It wasn't long before we heard sirens. Dad jumped in the truck and told me to stay put. When he returned, his face was as pale as a ghost. My father said, "Georgie boy, I can't talk about it now, your friend Patrick was badly hurt and he needs our prayers." He hugged me and went silent…The weekend arrived and rumors began. When the facts came out, I was told Patrick used a pipe bomb to break up ledge in order to anchor a supporting post. While adding gun powder to the pipe, there was friction, igniting a spark. The bomb blew up in Patrick's hands, also blowing out his intestines. Patrick tried desperately to put his insides back in place. He lay on the ground begging for help. In the early 1920s it was impossible to repair that kind of damage. With no antibiotics, the exposure killed him." In school days later, my friend Peter and I told our classmates it could have been us. Peter hadn't done his homework the night before and had to stay after school. Peter's nightmares began when he got to the shack before his best friend was carried away. Surely the image of Patrick crying out in pain has been permanently etched in his brain."

My father was a strong and resilient man who had many hard knocks in life. Our family went through more heartbreak than most families... His true legacy came after my brother's vicious murder at a routine traffic stop. Dad became acutely aware that the state needed tougher laws to protect our first line of defense. During the 1980s and 90s, he worked diligently to change the death penalty law. Back then, our officials and the laws had become more liberal, making it impossible for the bill to pass. He believed it needed to be reinstated for the killing of police officers... He also fought to stop first degree murderers from being allowed out on weekend passes. With my father's dedication and hard work, the second bill became law in Massachusetts. With the enactment of the new law, signed in 1988, murderers could no longer get weekend passes to kill again. At a State House ceremony in Boston, my father received an award for the work he accomplished. Dad was a dedicated man who loved and provided for his family. In spite of being a tough guy at times, he showed compassion along with exemplary strength to all.

If you don't recount your family history, it will be lost.
Honor your own stories and tell them, too.
The tales may not seem very important, but they are what
binds families and makes each of us who we are.

Madeleine Engle

A Mother's Broken Heart Concealed

Chapter 22

In 1984, just two years after my oldest brother George was killed in the line of duty, I overheard a conversation between Mom and my aunt. "Peg, how have you survived such tragedies? Your oldest son who brought you such love, pride and happiness throughout his short life—murdered in cold blood—killed with such brutal atrocity. I could not have lived through that!" said Aunt Beth. "I remember the years it took to have your first child. He was a beautiful 9 lb. boy, born with the cord wrapped around his neck causing still birth. A year later, God blessed you with your second son George, only to be returned back to Him at 36 years young." My aunt reached for mother's hand.

From the porch I noticed my aunt's tears and seemingly constrained face as she became speechless. My mother replied stoically; "Beth, a day doesn't go by that I don't grieve or shed tears for my children gone before me. In spite of these irreparable heartbreaks, I am blessed to have four remaining children who need me." She continued speaking to my aunt about the difficulties of burying four children at different stages of her life. "As you know, my

129

last children born were twins, John and Judith, both change of life babies. I'm sure you remember back in the 1950s, when Judith, my special Down syndrome baby, was born with a heart defect. John was a healthy boy weighing four pounds more than his twin sister. I still remember the doctor standing at my bedside giving me that fateful news. The doctor said. "More than likely, Judith would not make her first birthday." No matter how much they prepared me, it was impossible to comprehend—I wouldn't give up hope. Once home, my other five children instantly bonded with their new sister and brother. They called the twins; "Jack and Jill" and often enjoyed reciting the famous nursery rhyme…We were blessed to have our sweet baby Jill for eight months."

Mother also talked about the loss of her beautiful middle daughter who died by suicide back in the early 1970s at age 24. Sadly she revealed; "Martha's death left me with a different kind of broken and it greatly affected her dad. George had a nervous breakdown and it took time for us to recover." She also said, "It was after Martha's death that we felt the need to move out of our large family home. It completely knocked the wind out of us. The hard work of caring for a big home had become overwhelming. Our beautiful home, once filled with laughter, felt cold and empty. I have children who will never return and the rest have moved on. George Sr. retired, closing his business and change became essential."

Before making my appearance, I recall having similar feelings as my mother. At 35 years old, I was standing in the breezeway eavesdropping like a kid. I too felt that painful void of missing my siblings. Taking a deep breath, I joined them in a cup of tea and biscuits…Just as I thought, the subject changed. Left with more unanswered questions and the inability to express how these losses affected me, I went along with the new and more pleasant conversation.

I began to realize that, after my mother buried her oldest son, feelings of sadness were now permanently etched on her face. This was the fourth child my parents buried. So often I'd catch her gazing out the window as if she'd gone somewhere, lost in time. During family gatherings, Mother would keep busy, appearing as though she were feeling the joy of the holidays. I know now nothing was ever the same for her. She kept her sadness hidden because in those days she wanted to appear strong throughout these adversities. My mother wanted nothing but happiness for her remaining children, putting family first.

The years had taken its toll. Mother died from a broken heart in 1987, five years after her oldest son's murder. Right to the end, mother stood strong concealing her brokenness. My parents have been through the unimaginable horror of burying not one, not two but four beautiful children over the years. Just how was this possible for two people to walk this difficult journey? My dad always seemed buried in his work, remaining strong. Much of his survival depended on his belief that exercising both body and mind would see him through. This was his best answer.

For the first time in my life, I am walking in my mother's shoes. She passed away at 70, the same age I will be this year. Like her, I lost a daughter, my only child. Life as I've known it is no more. I am truly experiencing her deepest sorrow. Like she did, I find myself staring off—lost in time—more often than not. Each day I find myself putting one foot in front of the other, living with a broken heart concealed. I too am dealing with the ultimate tragedy, an out of order reality. Without this undying love for Laura, I could not feel the depths of despair. Remembering that fateful day when complicated grief entered my heart. The bags under my eyes will continue to store tears waiting to leak out at any given time. Any parent who has lost a child knows what complicated grief is. Our tears are different. These drops come from the heart and are expressions of emotions felt deep within the soul…Our heartfelt love is eternal.

A Grandparent's Precious Gift

Chapter 23

The memory of waiting for my first grandchild never fades. I recall the long night I paced the hallway, envisioning the worst! I tried composing myself once the nurse approached to say, "Laura is asking for her mom so please follow me." As I set foot in her room, my daughter appeared traumatized after a painful and exhausting delivery. I could almost feel the pain etched on her face. Without another word she said, "Mum, it's a boy!" Filled with excitement, I gave her a big hug, saying how proud I was. Her husband presented me with their precious gift, my grandson, now swaddled in my arms! I was walloped by a love so intense, like nothing I'd felt before.

I had a different feeling when I'd given birth to Laura. The love and joy felt equal, however being a young mother brought mixed emotions. So many overwhelming thoughts and emotions brought light to the obligations that lay ahead. Being a grandmother creates different feelings, giving me a second chance. Watching them grow while experiencing the joy with only a fraction of the responsibility. To sum it up, it's easier and more fun. My husband and I are allowed to spoil them, guilt-free while parents do the hard work. Their busy lives give us a chance to bond giving undivided attention. We can read an extra book or take them to the zoo on weekdays.

As an experienced grandmother with time to ponder, I've often wondered why the first word out of a toddler's mouth is "no" rather than "yes." My theory is a bit multifaceted. As parents or grandparents, we say "no" more often than any other word, especially when toddlers touch things they shouldn't. Our voices change, and the harsh sounding word sticks in their brain. It's also a sign that the terrible twos have arrived. Tots learn to say "no" quickly, especially when forced to eat something they don't want. In the early stages of self-awareness, children learn quickly how to maneuver in a world bigger than them.

As grandparents, we were fortunate to have lived near my daughter and grandchildren. When our grandson was a toddler and he said "no" to something, his immediate response was a smile that would melt anyone's heart. Of course whenever I insisted Johnny finish his squash, it would land on the floor or I'd wear that mustard-color vegetable spewed on my blouse! Whenever Mom asked him to pick up his toys, he'd run as far as he could laughing all the way. Mom or Dad would pursue with discipline, while I enjoyed coddling him. The energy Johnny had as a child has continued to be an asset throughout his life. He was a determined child who became a great athlete with a kind heart. No matter what sport, he challenged and excelled in every one. In school he wasn't much for the books, nevertheless, he was considered one of the best baseball players around. My husband spent time teaching him the game and the importance of practice. Johnny not only valued the lessons his grandfather taught him, he decided to be the best. We went to every game and watched the parents who knew his abilities. They'd park their cars far from the field. I recall a day when a man parked his new Lexus near the fence. He thought he was fortunate to have these parking spaces available coming late. To his surprise after the game, he found a small indent on his hood from one of Johnny's home runs, knocking another ball out of the park. He had the most hits out of all the school players for two years. Now married with a good career, he works hard meeting his potential. Of course being tall and handsome has proved to be a beneficial asset.

Our delightful granddaughter is on the quieter, gentler side, which made life easier for her mother. When Brooke was born, I felt the same emotions as I did with my grandson. A new chamber grew in my heart when I first held her. Again overwhelmed with euphoria! A forever place in my heart, permanently etched with love, for this perfect baby girl. I swooned and stared at her sweet face barely noticing she was born with no hair. Ironically her hair is thicker now than many other family members…Once Brooke began to sit with little support, she took a lot of nonsense from her 2-year-old brother. Mom would encourage Johnny to give kisses to his sister and most of the time he was gentle. Other times he'd clumsily kiss her quick, knocking her sideways or backwards. He seemed to know she was protected by many pillows. Still, Brooke would cry, generally because her feelings had been hurt. Like her mom, she walked at an early age. As steady as she was on her feet, Brooke needed protection from her little brother who often lurked nearby. And yes, a little hellion he was.

I watched Brooke overcome many obstacles through the years. She learned from a young age that if life was going to work out for her, she had to make it happen. Brooke was also determined, as she strived to be a healthy teen, always on top of her game. I recall one day watching her play softball when the batter hit a high fly, fast and furious. Brooke was reaching for the ball in the outfield with the sun directly in her eyes. Unable to protect her face in time, her nose took a direct hit in need of a doctor. The experienced coach had a bag of peas in her ice chest saving the day. She bravely finished the season out. In high school, she was captain of the volleyball team, doing a wonderful job. We enjoyed watching her games. Brooke put herself through collage and we expect she'll have a very lucrative career in the medical field, helping others.

In 2011, we were blessed with another grandson. By then, our other two were in their late teenage years. My stepson and his family live in Florida, almost three hours by plane. We don't see Mason as much as we'd like, however, he is thriving with the support of two loving parents. Thanks to social media, we keep up with all things he's involved in, using FaceTime. Not one of my favorite apps! As much as we love looking at Mason's youthful face, he sees two people rapidly aging on his end of the iPhone. For me, close-ups are disturbing yet funny! Mason is the bravest of all and we love to hear him tell exciting stories. His dad and mom have taken him to see so much of the world at a young age. He can hike for miles and rock climb higher than most kids his age. Mason can be quite a daredevil with little fear. He is also quite a hockey and soccer player. We hope to spend more time with our third grandchild before he too becomes a young adult living life to the fullest. We are truly blessed to have lived to watch two of them grow to be happy and healthy adults!

Grandparents are a delightful blend of laughter, caring deeds, wonderful stories and love.

Author Unknown

The Scarf in my Dream

Chapter 24

We all have stories to tell...For me, it's finding more adventures, more tales going forward, or so I've been told. All things considered, I love my drives down memory lane. It allows me the joy of running into those I've loved and lost...My youngest sister, however, rarely enjoys looking in the rear view mirror. She'd rather sail off looking for those glorious sunsets, relaxing under the tropical palm trees with a Pina colada in hand. In some ways, it's what sets two sisters apart—unique and different. I'm delighted going back in search of those happy memories. I can now write about them, making it incredibly cathartic.

I've often wondered, what is the driving force behind my writing? I firmly believe it's been a way to emerge from the ashes of many tragedies. When my first book was completed and published, I embraced it. I was finally able to express and share the best and worst moments of my life. I never chose to be a writer, yet somehow the writing found me. Somewhere deep within, I knew my story needed to be told. I also made sure my book would be written in such a way as to help others. Stories do not always come from tragedies, and many books are written to share funny and uplifting moments. Putting memories on paper not only keeps them alive, it preserves them for many generations.

A dear friend of mine has been inspirational. Beth kept a personal journal since childhood with over six decades of memories to look back upon.

I truly believe a life completed is to leave something behind. What better way than through the narratives we share? I often think of my dad who loved telling stories of our family's history. I'm certain he too would have written a book if he were alive today. My dad had a memory that held dates, times and names better than anyone—right up until his passing at 92. He shared many historic events that happened in our home town. Fortunately the town library recorded some of my father's historical recollections…I once heard him say; "when an elderly person dies, it's much like losing a library to a fire." Their journey is over and we can't get back those stories they once told.

When I look for reasons to continue writing, I think to myself; "Am I looking for ways of escaping for a while, or might it simply be a form of therapy?" No matter.., I'm doing what has brought me pleasure in a life full of untold stories. I believe we all have a purpose in life, with good and bad happenings from the time we are born. Much of our journey may seem insignificant, yet certain life experiences eventually surface over time. When our happier memories come to mind, we should embrace those moments, sharing whenever possible. When we feel sadness or pain connected to our past, these feelings can be expressed through writing.

My first experience with death was in 1958. I was 9 years old when I lost my baby sister. Jill was 8 months young, with a full life ahead of her. It was a gray morning when our dad sat all the children down. He said; "Jill is no longer with us, God wanted her back home to be with the angels." Dad continued with tears in his eyes; "We were blessed to have Jill, even for a short time. Our little angel is now with God in heaven." Being a second grader, there was no way to comprehend death. I remember feeling sad for some time as it resonated throughout the household. Looking back, my parents protected us from their pain as much as possible. Just the same, my memory holds on to my precious baby sister, no matter how much time passes. I can still visualize Jill with her rosy cheeks, dark silky hair, dressed in a yellow flowered dress. I often wonder what my baby sister would look and be like today.

Another shocking tragedy was the day I lost another sister to suicide, two weeks after her 24th birthday, in 1974. Being a 27-year-old, I had some understanding of death but not of someone who has taken their own life. It was a hard thing for anyone to wrap their head around. There were so many feelings I was dealing with. I went from tears that wouldn't stop to a deep sense of sadness that lingered for years. I remember being consumed with guilt because as a family we failed to save her. Feelings of shame would also appear out of nowhere. I realized over time these feelings were happening because I was alive and not my sister. Families are shattered after this type of death and most are left with little to no support. They are never given the chance to make things right or say goodbye. Although it's never less painful when a loved one dies from cancer, there's already been a confrontation of losing that person. It gives families time to go through the grieving process. Many survivors of suicide are shell shocked. They live behind walls of silence due to the stigma attached to the act itself—not healthy and most difficult!

Right when life seemed to be going smoothly, my parents received a devastating call the night of February 26, 1983. A State Police cruiser pulled up to their house the night I was visiting. With a solemn look, a Trooper said to my dad, "Please let me escort you and your family to the hospital, your son has been shot." My knees buckled and I'm certain my parents felt similar sensations. We were in a state of shock. The Trooper didn't have much more information, however he drove us to St. Vincent's hospital, 40 minutes away. It was the longest and most painful ride of our lives. Upon arrival, the anxious feelings began taking my breath away. As we walked through the entrance, it was like entering a movie scene. Uniformed State Troopers along with men in trench coats were everywhere. My mind and body seemed to go numb and lifeless, as if floating by them. Two detectives asked us to follow them to the elevator where one could hear a pin drop. I made eye contact with one gentleman while shaking my head, "no'—it was a look he understood. He knew I was asking if my brother was alive. That was when he shook his head" "no," bringing his head and eyes slowly downward. The realization hit me—I had to be strong for my parents. Once the door opened, a familiar voice could be heard down the hall—a female sobbing hysterically. Reality for me had finally set in. My sister-in-law was with my brother who had already passed. We were all asked to join her, and without hesitation, my brave mother went to her son. I stayed with my dad who didn't have the will to see his firstborn son cold, bloody and lifeless. Quite honestly, neither could I. My big brother had been shot multiple times during a routine traffic stop. No one knew how serious it was until we spoke with the doctor. Everything after that was a blur—my oldest brother, who always protected me—was now gone…For some odd reason, I wanted to hold on to his boots trying to fill some of that empty space for my younger siblings. I realized no one could ever fill them in the way he did.

I'm slowly learning each time a tragic event occurs, such as a sudden death of a love one, the worst place to be is in a state of denial. Although it's a natural defense and an immediate protection from present danger, it's only useful for a short time. If denial is left in place, other emotions find ways of burying themselves only to reappear in a negative way when least expected.

When mother passed away four years after losing her oldest son, the family knew the cause. As strong and brave as she was, her heart could not be repaired. It had shattered too many times. The gentle matriarch was the glue that kept our family together. We all knew when we lost her, we were on our own. Through all our adversities, we learned a great deal from both parents. Most importantly, they lead us to a higher power for guidance during difficult times. Mom's unwavering strength went far beyond what most others could endure in a lifetime.

A strange thing happened when I lost my mother. When she died suddenly, I helped my dad handle the funeral arrangements. From then on it was about keeping my mind and body in constant motion. Much of my time was invested in raising my daughter, helping my father and working as much as possible. Being busy meant I didn't have to face the pain of losing the most important person in my lifetime. As we sat in church the day of mother's funeral, feelings of grief flowed through the veins of all of us. After her burial, the denial stage for me was worse than ever. Unconsciously I was suppressing feelings…As time marched on, this became a problem. I hadn't dealt with the emotional loss—I wasn't able to said goodbye. Guilt was one feeling I couldn't shake. After all, why wasn't I able to grieve for my mother? Something was wrong with me. Sure enough, my life spun out of control and panic attacks began to occur. My world became smaller and I was close to becoming agoraphobic.

After several months of counseling, I was told I had developed a form of Post-Traumatic Stress Disorder. I came to realize there was a barricade keeping me from mourning my mother's death. I had been living in total denial in order to keep from feeling the same pain I experienced losing my three siblings. I refused to be treated with medications so I agreed to cognitive therapy. For me it was about understanding the problem. With time and work, brick by brick, I'd taken down the wall of denial and the panic attacks slowly dissipated, becoming non-existent.

The real healing began one night in a dream...

It was a dark and drizzly evening when out of the blue, I saw a woman walking toward the train station. She was dressed in a familiar trench coat, wearing a soft flowered scarf, tied under her chin. It appeared to be the train station at the bottom of the hill, close to where our family once lived. In my dream I was drawn toward her, trying to get a glimpse through the drizzle and dense fog. Just under the dim streetlight, she turned my way, ever so briefly. In spite of the thick mist, I saw a familiar smile as the lady in the scarf gently waved. It was then that I began feeling energized—"who was this person?" No matter how fast I walked, she remained at a distance. I couldn't seem to catch up. I picked up the pace to a jog but still to no avail.

After realizing one of my shoelaces came untied, I bent down to quickly tie it. When I looked up in her direction, in what seemed like seconds, she was gone. Below, the train slowly began moving away from the station making that loud familiar sound. I felt sure the lady with the scarf boarded the train. As the conductor blew the distinctive loud horn... I awoke from my dream.

The next morning, an uncanny thing happened!

As I rummaged through my lingerie drawer for a pair of nylon stockings, I noticed a familiar item tucked in the back corner. To my amazement.., it was the scarf in my dream. Did my mother lead me to her delicate scarf through a dream? I knew this discovery was the sign I needed. It was then that my healing began. My beautiful mother came to me in a dream, to say good-bye...

"No daughter and mother ever live apart, no matter what the distance between them."

Christie Watson

Hearts Intertwined

Chapter 25

The bond between mother and child is something almost mystical—a love that is unconditional with the passage of time. What a special joy when a mother hears her baby's heartbeat for the first time, or when she holds her infant after giving birth, affirming her love and commitment. For me, hearing the sounds of my daughter's first cry brought on the realization this little infant was totally dependent upon me. I became the center of my daughter's world where there is complete trust in every way…Two hearts intertwined.

In just a few short years of close nurturing, the time arrives when a mother's child begins first day of school. It's a time when they both experience their first separation, that tugging at the heart kind of feeling.

While thoughts emerge, I reflect on those awe-inspiring memories of my own mother. Her endless love and devotion always spread out equally amongst her children. I found that same undying love when I gave birth to my daughter. Having my mother in my life for 38 years was a blessing, although it wasn't long enough. She was with us through my daughter's preschool and teenage years when I needed her most.

After my daughter Laura started her first day of school, Mother and I shared memories of my first day, over coffee and blueberry scones. She reminded me of my stubbornness when I was told I'd be wearing a catholic school uniform. I guess having a temper tantrum was not an uncommon strategy for me. After all, tom boys were not fond of wearing plaid skirts and knee-high socks, especially on a daily basis. Mother somehow had a special way of calming me. Her reassuring words were, "Molly, develop friendships at school and once home, change back into your play clothes. Think of it the same way as how your name changes from Mary to Molly when home." It worked! On my first day, mother introduced me to my first grade teacher, waiting to greet me. I still recall that dreadful feeling when Mary first met Sr. Anita.

Being an inquisitive, hyperactive 5-year-old couldn't have been easy on my mother. Having a brother a few years older taught me how to be a bit rough and tough around the edges. Georgie and I loved pushing ourselves to the limit playing ball, in hide and seek, and racing our bicycles to see who could go the fastest. We loved the noise our baseball cards made on our spokes using Mother's clothes pins…There were lots of bumps and bruises along the way, surely provoking many anxious moments for her… I can clearly remember a scary incident back when my brother Georgie was playing at a friend's house. He came shrieking from the neighbor's basement holding his eye. One of the older boys had been shooting a BB gun when one of the BB's ricocheted off the cement wall hitting my brother in the eye. Mother came to the rescue, racing to get her son to the hospital. As it turned out, it lodged in the inner corner of his eye. Once removed, my mother was told her son was one lucky boy! There were no lasting effects, just utter relief Georgie hadn't lost an eye.

I have a vivid recall of a cold New England winter in 1954. That year was particularly stormy and I had come down with a high fever. By then, antibiotics had become widely available for the use of curing diseases caused by bacterial infections. The doctor had arrived at our home, diagnosing me with scarlet fever. Before penicillin, this disease had killed many people until the great discovery. In spite of this miraculous drug, I was a very sick girl. My fever spiked to 104 and I clearly remember being in horrific pain. Unless the room was dark, my eyes stayed closed due to any painful light source. My face felt like it was burning up. I went from sweating to shivering in a matter of minutes. My lymph nodes were extremely swollen, both in my neck and groin area and it hurt to move my legs. The rash had spread over my entire body, I felt hot and itchy and I could barely swallow. Mother kept my other siblings away, for fear of it spreading. The comfort of having her near had removed some of the pain and anxiety.

I'm sure my mother now has the most beautiful angel wings for all she had done for her family. She not only tended to all my needs, she tended to my 8-year-old brother, my two sisters who were 4 and 5, as well as one toddler and a set of infant twins. My mother's hands were full, nevertheless she barely left my side. During the first 48 hours, she slept with me, never letting her worry show. I also remember the doctor making a few house calls. Before leaving after his initial visit, he taped a sign to the outside of my closed door that read, *Quarantined*! How grateful my parents were when none of the other family members got sick. Mother did everything to protect them. After a week passed, I began feeling better and was allowed to reunite with family.

How blessed I was to have such a loving mother. All the worrying she did, kissing and bandaging all her children's boo-boo's. Her unique ways of taking away those painful moments of hurt and sadness are remembered. No matter how sick or how much trouble we were in, she was there to nurture, understand and to listen with enduring love without judgement.

My own experience as a mom is a special bond that spans forever. It's a lifelong relationship that can be both difficult and rewarding. There will be times of drifting apart as daughters seek independence, however, the deep bond remains. For me, the appreciation for my mother has grown through time. She's been gone from my life for over 30 years but remains forever in my heart. This close relationship with my mother allowed me to be a loving mom to my own lifelong friend, my beautiful daughter...

In loving memory of my dear mother,

Margaret V. Flaherty Hanna

My Dream in a Time Machine

Chapter 26

Surrounded by a sea of fog, I found myself inside an odd-shaped machine. A sense of calmness flowed through my body knowing somehow I'd be taken to a street called Memory Lane. Resting my head back on a shiny colored metallic seat, I began observing this powerful machine, a peculiar looking vehicle. Shaped like a missile with one door and one seat, it had an oblong-shaped wheel with a button in the middle. Oddly enough, my hands began gripping this steering wheel that wouldn't move. The realization set in: I was in a Time Machine. A bit hesitant, I pushed the only button that was flashing a ghastly green color. In the blink of an eye, there I was, being transported back to those carefree days as a child. Arriving at my destination seemed to take little time. I was ecstatic at the thought of revisiting my favorite places of yesteryear. To once again go back and see all of us in our younger years, including my dearly departed loved ones. It felt like a miracle in progress. These adventures would hopefully include those pleasurable vacations, bringing back my fondest of memories.

Growing up, my parents loved renting oceanfront cottages in summer. These were great times in spite of the inevitable obstacles that happen to everyone. Mary's first stop was to visit the family's fairytale cottage back in 1955.

Upon arrival, the siblings were playing games together while Mother cooked breakfast. That day, everyone spent time at the beach while Dad found himself painting the outside trim. The summer cottage sat secluded, high above the rocks. That evening was the first time noticing the nearby lighthouse casting an amber glow upon the gray shingles. Whenever the waves slammed into the rocks below, it sounded like thunder beneath the sea. As beautiful as this place was, the upkeep disagreed with our dad. It wasn't long before he found ownership unrewarding. The cottage had sold within a week. Nevertheless, my visit allowed me to begin solidifying those days of yore.

My second stop was to the campgrounds in Truro on Cape Cod, late 1950s. Owning a camper was popular in those days and a great way to travel. Dad purchased a brand new Winnebago that was big and comfy, suitable to sleep a family of eight. The grounds were just as I remembered and the ocean was close enough to hear the waves crashing. Next to the campground was the once popular Drive-In where older kids were still seen hanging over the fence catching a peek. During late hours, shady movies would be shown and the boys continued getting caught. The attraction wasn't just what was played on the big screen, there was action adventure right inside some of the vehicles.

A painful event appeared before me and I was about to relive it again. Prior to the family heading for the cape, my older brother Georgie was clowning around while I was drinking out of a glass Coca-Cola bottle. He came from behind pushing it against my teeth. I began crying from the impact that eventually calmed down. Once in Wellfleet, I felt a dull pain above my tooth that lingered. My mother found a store carrying miniature like pillows to place between my lip and tooth to numb the pain. This worked until it fell out while jumping over the waves. It wasn't long before I screamed in agony as the sharp pain shot up into my nose. Sensing my pain, Dad drove me all over the upper Cape looking for a weekend dentist, an almost impossible task. Being a police officer, he had a knack of finding people. After what seemed hours, dad's wagon screeched to a halt. He spotted a sign hanging on the shingles of an old cape-style home. Relief came over his face after seeing a dentist's name inscribed on it. After several knocks on both doors, a gruffly mannered fellow finally answered.

Subsequently, seeing me in distress with a swollen face, he said, "Use the side door and I'll see what I can do." After taking pictures of the tooth, he asked, "Did you bang your tooth in recent days?" I still can't recall if I tattled on my brother however, relief came when the dentist put a temporary medication inside the tooth. I'll never forget those frightening words when the dentist finished. "Your front tooth will die, eventually turning black." Because I was revisiting, I thought to myself, "what an impact his statement must have left me, a young 10-year-old girl!"

From the moment my eyes opened, I realized the time machine had only existed in my dream. It became clear, these machines truly are fictional. However, our memories forever belong to us and no one can take them away. We

153

can alter past events by choice or by how we recollect what happened. I also understand at least for me, the need to find my way back. Too many painful losses without goodbyes brings yearning for the "before it happened" when things were good. Also, as wonderful as it might be to revisit the past, life must go forward making new memories.

As this chapter continues, my memories will be written in *real* time.

Awake and reminiscing Mary's favorite summer place...

Our family's first stay in Duxbury was in summer of '71 when my dad found a rare but beautiful oceanfront rental. Everyone looked forward to spending time together at the ocean. The three oldest were married with families of their own. George, Martha and I were the oldest and eager to watch our girls making sandcastles in the sand. No one knew the time spent in Duxbury would be the last vacation our family as a whole would spend together.

When Saturday morning arrived, the younger siblings jumped in the family wagon filled to the brim with boxes of food, plenty of sunscreen, stacks of towels, clothes and extra bathing suits. Mother also made sure she packed a first aid kit, calamine lotion and a jar of Noxzema for sunburns. No sooner had they arrived when the children grabbed their bathing suits and headed for the beach. The older siblings along with our partners and children arrived later that afternoon.

The large year-round house was filled with cottage-style furniture and enough bedrooms to accommodate everyone. The younger boys chose to sleep on cots pressed against the walls of a wraparound porch with its panoramic views. There in Duxbury, I had discovered sleeping with the windows open was an absolute must! Hearing the waves rhythmically crashing, the squawking seagulls searching for food and the sound of a distant fog horn brought inner feelings of tranquility. I also felt it was there in Duxbury that I'd found a special joy in reconnecting with family. It became my happy place and I knew one day, I'd find my way back...

Years passed and although I held on to dreams of going back, it seemed to be just that. To find time or money for vacation was nearly impossible. Rentals on the waterfront were not affordable to a divorced, struggling mother. Nevertheless, I never let my fantasy fade regardless of life's difficulties and for me it was anything but easy.

Heartbreak and life altering events began taking their toll. Two years after the wonderful family gathering, I lost my beautiful sister Martha to suicide in 1973. For the family it was a profound loss. I'll always wonder what life could have been like, having my sister to grow old with. Martha and I had only begun creating a bond. Seasons come and go, however that empty space in my heart forever remains. Ten years later, in 1983, my oldest brother George was brutally murdered, leaving another hole with deeply embedded scars...Due to a broken heart, I lost my beautiful mother unexpectedly in 1987. Complete recovery from these types of tragic losses is unlikely, and for my mom, as strong as she was, recovery wasn't possible.

In the late 1980s, I found myself driving in the direction of Duxbury beach to once again recapture memories of happier times. My day trips were spent strolling along the beach, making sure to pass by that special place. Walking barefoot and soaking up the sunshine allowed the soothing gentle waves to quell my deep sadness. It wasn't long before I noticed what appeared to be an abandoned cottage by the sea. That was it, the memorable place once filled with family, joy and laughter. I found myself once again piecing together those wonderful moments from the summer of '71. If only there really was a time machine making it possible to go back—reliving precious times— just once!

New Beginnings

It was late autumn of '91, when I heard the news that a storm had passed through Duxbury, devastating the beaches and properties along the southern coast. The *"No Name Storm"* caused beach erosion and heavily damaged properties including the famous *Gurnet Inn,* which was never rebuilt. The waterfront cottage my parents rented 20 years earlier was nearby. It sustained minimal damage compared to the surrounding cottages. The gentleman that once rented the cottage to our family was now quite elderly. Mr. Johnson sold the cottage, allowing the new owners to do an extensive remodel, making it their attractive year-round home.

During that same year, I met a wonderful man and it was love at first sight. It was a whirlwind relationship playing tennis, dancing and spending time together with family. We were married in 1992. Due to Bill's long working hours, we thoroughly enjoyed getting away every summer. Our first years were filled with adjustments as we began our marriage combining families. My only daughter was grown and married and Bill's three boys were not living with us. The two oldest were in their late teens, however Bill's 12-year-old spent time with us on weekends and holidays. In 1995, my daughter Laura and her husband blessed us with our first grandson John Jr... The following year we were blessed again with a beautiful granddaughter named Brooke.

It was important for me to find my way back to Duxbury to begin a new family tradition. One day while walking the beach with my husband, we saw a rental sign on the side of a porch. It was a gorgeous year-round house overlooking the ocean, completely rebuilt due to the '91 storm. I knew the owners from my home town and arranged to rent during the month of July each year. An agreement was signed and the new tradition began for my family. Over the next 20-plus years, everyone got to know each other in the friendly community, mostly due to the awesome 4th celebrations which included cookouts, bonfires, and the long awaited spectacular fireworks. It's an indescribable scene seeing the uninterrupted burst of colors exploding up and down the beach each year. Duxbury became a continuance of happy times making memories. Every year the grandkids made sure they spent every moment possible with us. Our family loves sharing hilarious stories of past—with hope it continues on through generations—truly a blessing!

Sometimes life's scary moments return now and then, testing our strength and endurance. It was the year 2016 when the family had another frightening event. On the last day of vacation, I was getting things packed so that Bill could fill up the SUV. He enjoyed his time loading and unloading the vehicle. It's a sad day for everyone when it means leaving the beach behind. The grandkids always slept in the last day, not wanting to leave. With just a few hours left, I finished packing my suitcase and headed down stairs. Approaching the front door, I noticed my husband sitting by the window appearing pale and tired. This was not like him—my husband always got things zipped up and done ahead of time. He casually mentioned he needed a minute to sit as he had a little pain similar to his past gallbladder attacks. Bill blamed it on the large bagel and cream cheese he just finished. Thing was, his gallbladder had been taken out years ago. Now concerned, I woke my grandkids, conveying the urgency for them to carry everything out to the vehicle. I'm sure they saw the worried look on my face. After things were loaded in the vehicles, everyone headed back home. Bill seemed quiet, not mentioning his discomfort till that evening and again next morning. Both times I suggested he go to the ER. Finally mid-day I insisted we go to the hospital. Strangely, he didn't resist. Once the tests were done, the doctor entered the ER cubical saying, "Bill, your enzymes show you are having a heart attack." He was immediately taken to the ICU where the medical team prepared him for one or more stents the next day. It was another long and anxious time. Just when happiness found me with this wonderful man in my life, I knew all too well how quickly things change.

There I was, pacing in the waiting room praying silently. By late afternoon I was allowed to see my husband. Bill was wide awake asking the doctor when he could get back to work. I couldn't believe my ears but then again, yes I could—he was going to be alright.

The doctor looked at us and said, "He was one lucky man! Bill, you were well on your way to the "widow maker" heart attack. It's the type of heart attack where there's no coming back. Your blockage was just over 96% in the main artery."   Reflecting back to that morning at the beach and the long drive home with Bill at the wheel, I truly believe God took over the steering that day. He knew I would not survive another tragic death. There's a saying, *God doesn't give us more than we can handle.* "Believe me, I have questioned Him more than once..."

Bill's recovery went well and family continues to enjoy their happy place at Duxbury Beach. I truly feel the best gift bestowed on us is God's gift of extra time making memories! The grandchildren, now young adults, continue vacationing with their grandparents. No matter how many years pass, those who are drawn to a happy place will once again find their way back.

'A Vacation is like love – anticipated with pleasure, and remembered with nostalgia.'

Author Unknown

A Mother's Life Shattered

~ Memories of My Lovely Daughter ~

Chapter 27

My beautiful and spirited Laura was unique in so many ways. From the time she was born, she marched to the beat of her own drum. Although short lived, Laura refused to crawl during those early months. She was happiest standing up, gripping her little fingers around mine. Her chubby legs and feet were always in motion. This demanded lots of time and attention due to Laura's untiring energy and determination right from the start.

Looking back, holding her tiny hands while she took her first steps, is a memory treasured. Around 7 months, she began pulling away, walking from table to chair, kitchen to living room, no matter how many times she fell. Laura persisted until she walked on her own, weeks later. There were instances when she'd fall down, only to find her frightened little face dissolve into a smile. During toilet training, Laura would refuse to remain seated on the commode, especially when she found herself fixated on the bowl beneath her. That's when Mother took to bribery. Along with running a little water, I'd place a large red apple on the sink telling Laura she'd win the prize if she would tinkle. Because she wanted to bite into that big apple, she was trained long before other toddlers her age. This was my beautiful daughter from the very start— tenacious, stubborn and funny. Laura somehow managed to keep her bottle at bedtime, much longer than the doctor's recommendation. Otherwise, a night's sleep wasn't possible. As a little girl, Laura loved taking over conversations with grown-ups, especially family. And oh how she loved the attention! If there were guests or parties at our home, she wanted to know everyone, often filling the room with laughter. As an only child, hanging around adults contributed to Laura achieving independence in her early years.

Life was good for my little girl, until her 10th birthday party... Her dad wasn't there to celebrate her special day. We had gone through a messy divorce and it was difficult on Laura. Her father remarried, moved to another state and had two more children. He and his second wife created a new life which didn't include his first daughter. It was during this time that her father became absent in Laura's life. The support of family helped compensate for the void she felt.

Together, both Laura and I went through more than our share of life's difficulties. Thankfully she had a special connection to her late grandmother, "Nanny." She also loved her Aunt Martha and Uncle Georgie who both died tragically. These losses created emotional unrest and anxiety issues for the two of us. Without her dad, Laura's Nanny had become her substitute parent.

When Laura entered first grade, her Aunt Martha had been going through unfortunate circumstances, as well as suffering from depression. This left Martha feeling helpless and hopeless. Sadly, family members were unable to help her. In May of 1974, she died by suicide in our home. No one knew the depth of Martha's pain or that it would be her last visit and silent goodbye. She had overdosed on her newly prescribed antidepressant medication and did not survive in spite of desperate attempts. This is one of those tragically misunderstood deaths. Looking back, I remember our home had been filled with turmoil and trauma that day, all witnessed by my little girl. I still don't know how that affected Laura, except we went through this nightmare together. Just as we did 10 years later, when her Uncle George was shot and killed in the line of duty. There were many traumatic experiences that began when her father walked away, never to look back. Both my sister's and brother's deaths were impacts, leaving me emotionally unavailable to my daughter during my most difficult times. These tragic events were completely out of our control.

I truly believe the most difficult loss for Laura, at 19 years of age, was when her "Nanny" died unexpectedly. After losing her grandmother, she developed anxiety and an eating disorder, most likely due to Post Traumatic Stress. Laura received immediate counseling and healing began to take place for her. Just before her 21st birthday, I had broken the horrific news that her dad had died—also by suicide, leaving yet another impact.

———————

As a young girl, one of Laura's survival mechanisms was her love and affection for animals. While growing up, she had her fair share of untrained dogs and outdoor cats. Taking care of animals is how she channeled her energy. When Laura was 11, she and her best friend, Kristin, would sneak over to a nearby farm to visit the horses. In time, the prominent veterinarian who owned the many acres of farmland allowed Laura and Kristin to groom, feed and muck out the horse stalls. She enjoyed being around them, taking excellent care responsibly. On her own, Laura found something she loved to do and it was the best therapy ever. She had fallen head over heels for one particular horse named Pinto. They had a special way of communicating, making it an unforgettable love story. Besides the occasional apples and carrots, Laura would sneak him a lifesaver. When he'd see her coming, Pinto would proudly hold his head high and whinny. When she got close, he would knicker or blow gently through his nostrils, happy to see her. Every day, he patiently waited for his friend and if she didn't have any lifesavers, he certainly let her know!

Of course being a mom, there were many periods of worry. Surely there were times I overreacted, making things worse. There was one particular recollection when Laura came through the door with swollen eyes nearly shut. After speaking with her doctor, it was determined to be an allergic reaction, most likely due to the stray cats and other animals living in the barn. Nothing would stop Laura, even if she couldn't see out of those swollen slits. She wasn't going to give up her love for horses and, ironically, she outgrew the allergy.

Like so many other young girls in the 1970s, she and Kristin didn't mind mucking out stalls daily. This was done in exchange for riding lessons. The proprietor of the farm adored Laura, allowing her to ride his favorite horse, Pinto. As she got to know and care for these horses, the owners taught her dressage, preparing her and Pinto for Show. With time and hard work, Laura learned to ride, allowing her to enter different horse shows and win blue ribbons.

When Laura was ready for the big time horse shows, I'd be there with camera in hand. For Laura it wasn't always easy having her mother there, knowing I was a worrywart. To prove her right, there were two shows never to be forgotten. It was Laura's first dressage competition held locally, and she was feeling both excited and nervous. Her anxiety went through the roof when we discovered she didn't have her number yet. Without a word, Laura handed me Pinto's reins and took off like a jack rabbit... There I stood, holding on to the tallest, broadest horse ever—scared and shaky knowing I was in control of a horse… I had never let on I was terrified of these mammoth animals. You see, to save face, Laura never knew I was kicked by one as a kid. As I held on to his rein, my heart began pounding through my chest, exceeding well over 100 beats a minute. If Pinto hadn't stayed calm, there was no doubt I would've run for the hills! Thank goodness Laura returned lickety-split, otherwise she might have discovered my phobia of horses.

The second and scariest time was when I attended the Endurance Riding Event Laura had entered. Unbeknownst to me, someone from the farm had switched Laura to a different horse. Pinto and his owner were scheduled for a parade that day. Even though this new horse was magnificent looking, I realized Laura and this gigantic stallion would be jumping as part of the event. My adrenalin began surging and I was filled with distress. I knew Laura wasn't quite experienced enough. Kristin had informed me that neither of them had ever ridden Challenger, who was a steeplechase horse. As I watched helplessly in the stands, my mind and body entered into the fight or flight mode. I was experiencing intense anxiety. My daughter, who was just 13 at the time, headed into the woods well in control of the horse. When she came galloping out, which seemed like forever, relief was immediately taken over by fear. I noticed her saddle seemed to be leaning to the right. Without further ado, the horse began to circle toward the jump in what seemed seconds. Laura's body began sliding sideways with the saddle. As she tried to correct herself, she went backwards during the jump, landing hard on her back. I ran to her like a wild animal saving her young. Again I felt my heart racing, only this time it was well over 200 beats per minute. It seemed like forever before the officials let her get up. Laura claimed she was fine and seemed intact as she walked back to the barn area. Even though I insisted we go to the ER, she protested, affirming she was fine.

As time marched on, Laura experienced occasional back pain without complaint. Old injuries tend to surface, causing problems later in life, as it had for Laura in her 40s. After finally having x-rays due to back pain, the doctor reported arthritis had developed from an old spine injury.

Being young and in love with horses, nothing deterred Laura from getting back in the saddle, riding the trails with her best friend. I must say my own fears melted away whenever I saw my daughter's face light up when riding Pinto. Her determination and hard work to ride and be with the Appaloosa made me proud. Laura was so prideful of Pinto and the ribbons she won. Laura's best memories were those days on the farm, learning to ride horses. She often talked about her love for Pinto, right up until her passing 36 years later. Horseback riding and her love for animals contributed to Laura's strength through the many adversities in her lifetime.

Just recently, Laura's childhood friend Kristin reached out through messenger. She shared with me a fond memory that made her smile... She wrote, "It was the first snowfall of the season. Laura and I couldn't get to the farm fast enough. Once there, we walked Pinto and Josh out from the barn with smiles on our faces. Without hesitation, we grabbed the reins and some mane while mounting rather awkwardly. Riding bareback, felt as if we were on rocking horses. I remember how happy we were, cantering through the snowy fields, laughing ourselves silly."

In her teen years, Laura had the normal ups and downs, as did many of her friends. More often than not, we found laughter together when issues arose. There were times as a mother I felt as though I was on a roller coaster ride. The good news is that Laura never looked for trouble although on occasion, it found her. In many ways, much like me growing up. She did well in school, had many friends and thankfully, stayed away from drugs. In her late teens and early 20s, Laura took college courses and continued to enjoy socializing with her high school friends. Laura's personality was generally upbeat and she could make anyone laugh. Her best qualities had been her sense of humor, quick wit and sharp edge. As Laura tried to process the loss of her dad and loved ones as a young adult, she kept those sad feelings locked inside. These negative emotions were covered up by her beautiful smile and contagious laughter.

Happiness found Laura when she met her soulmate at 23. Her husband to be, a tall handsome gentleman, came to me asking for her hand in marriage. They married soon after and purchased their first house in Laura's hometown. It wasn't long after her second child was born that she was diagnosed with postpartum depression. This was difficult for her because she struggled with anxiety and depression. For years she self-medicated like many mothers at the end of each day. Laura looked for ways to unwind and feel better. During her marriage, she found it difficult keeping her anxiety under control. It was stressful juggling her work and family obligations. At times she would have panic attacks often happening while on the job. She tried prescribed medications, however most caused negative side effects.

Laura not only inherited her dad's tall slim build and green eyes, she also inherited his genetics for depression. The two days she felt most blessed in life were when she gave birth to her two children. In spite of her struggles, she loved being a mom. It was when they were teenagers that Laura's mood swings were more noticeable, causing chaos at times. As young adults, her kids began to understand their mother's difficulties. She loved them more than life. She'd often say, "I'd give up my own life to save either of my children."

During the last years of Laura's life, she was often in pain. She developed a host of issues, including Fibromyalgia and Peripheral Neuropathy, which some doctors believed were a result of years of untreated Lyme disease. In her mid-forties, Laura developed a fatal condition called Pulmonary Hypertension with a five-year survival rate. This condition affected her heart and lungs. She had a fairly rare form that not only took away her quality of life, she was unable to breath without oxygen near the end. Laura rarely complained, although due to her disabilities, she often expressed how useless she felt, unable to contribute to the family financially.

For Laura, family was most important. Because of the love and support, she worked hard trying to overcome the challenges in her life. As her mother, I had an uncanny sixth sense that I would somehow outlive my beautiful daughter. Mostly due to a devastating dream that replayed in my mind and tugged at my heart for years—seemingly to seal this fate that one day I would lose her. Laura would often say to others, "If my mom dies, there better be a six-foot hole dug for me next to her." She always felt she wouldn't survive another loss. I can only say these deepest feelings came from her many losses at a young age. Family and friends came and left, but the two of us had an unbreakable bond. Sadly on occasion she would also say; "Mom, I'm not strong like you." Laura never realized her own strengths, especially with all she endured.

A nightmare never forgotten… I can still recall jumping out of a sound sleep by a horrific dream in my late 20s. A nightmare no parent wants to have or remember. Looking back, I now believe it was a premonition. It was both frightening and surreal. We are not supposed to dream someone actually dies or is dead, especially our child. In this nightmarish abyss, my daughter drowned under the ice frozen pond I was standing on. There I was, looking down at her frightened and frozen face before waking in panic. The bad dream not only took my breath away, it stayed with me, remaining in the back of my mind.

The sad irony—Laura passed away due to lack of oxygen before her 50th birthday. Her death was caused by the late stages of pulmonary hypertension.

Rest in Peace my beautiful Laura...
May you continue your ride on Pinto, flying high with the
angels.
One day we'll fly together, united once again.

My Red Winged Visitors

Photo by *Ken Fitzgerald*

Chapter 28

"A Cardinal is a representative of a loved one who has passed. When you see one, it means they are visiting you. They usually show up when you most need them or miss them. They also make an appearance during times of celebration as well as despair to let you know they will always be with you. Look for them, they'll appear."

Author Unknown

~ INTRODUCTION ~

*My life-changing encounters—death no longer separates us—there is a hereafter. My story reveals how **my red***

*winged visitors—along with a miraculous **apparition**—*
saved my life.

Visitations are God's work. When our loved one dies, their
soul remains, allowing love and energy to continue. Their
spiritual being remains, if we are aware and open. Living
without my daughter wasn't possible without prayer and
the power of God delivering His messengers.

It was the day after the funeral. I awoke feeling
uncertain I'd make it through the day. Sleep had eluded me
due to the painful shock of burying my one and only child.
My beautiful daughter, Laura, was five months away from
her 50th birthday.

Once in bed that evening, I began feeling deep gratitude
for my husband. It was his strength and my unwavering
faith that I was now drawing upon. Just after midnight, I
found myself tossing and turning. Overwhelmed by grief,
the anxiety engulfed my very existence. The emotional pain
had come in waves, taking my breath away with each
sorrowful thought. Tears flowed with this intense yearning
for my daughter. It was as though she vaporized into thin
air, never to be seen again. This realization felt as if a large
wave struck, pulling me into the open sea. Again I
struggled to breathe—the unimaginable had happened. My
future and the life I once knew was taken from me in a
flash. In desperation, I asked God for strength to persevere
and for a sign my Laura was with Him in eternal life. As I

lay in bed, my eyes wouldn't close. I found myself staring at the clock. The minutes crept by as I continued hopelessly in prayer. Out of sheer exhaustion, I fell asleep around 5 a.m... Once daybreak arrived, I leaped out of bed due to those dark thoughts invading my head. I was ill prepared for the anguish I was experiencing. Even though I'd been through many tragic events, losing my daughter was one I wasn't sure I'd survive.

Just as I finished making the bed that morning, outside the window I noticed a red bird flapping his wings in the pine tree, trying to draw my attention. This elegant cardinal slowly flew to the nearby apple tree, as if trying to approach me. The red bird perched on the nearest branch, proudly cocking his head from side to side. As I moved closer and sat on the edge of the bed, we stared at one another for what seemed minutes. It happened to be a gloomy day with rain in the forecast. All of a sudden the dark billowy clouds seemed to separate, allowing just enough sun to peek through. These rays gave this exquisite cardinal the most brilliant red color as he gracefully flew away. It was at that moment that I felt a warm and calming presence. I knew this to be a messenger from heaven, giving me the strength to carry on. My beautiful Laura let me know she was out of pain and distress—I believe God had set her free.

This comforting event carried me throughout that day. However the days, nights, weeks, and months following would have challenged the bravest! Nights turned into days—days into nights—living became a struggle. I would find myself walking back and forth in the house, sometimes crying out, "why?"! Other times I'd find myself screaming out her name, hoping to feel my daughter's presence. During those difficult days, I was partially aware of these outbursts and indeed relieved that my doors and windows were shut.

Growing up, our family suffered several tragic losses far greater than the normal family. I remember being a second grader when my beautiful baby sister, Jill, died from pneumonia at 8 months young. It was less than two decades later when my younger sister, Martha, died by suicide at 24. In 1983, my brother George, 36, a Massachusetts State Trooper, was killed in the line of duty, brutally shot seven times.

During those dark periods when our family lost loved ones, I tried to be steadfast, the one everyone leaned on. This allowed me to remain strong because, as a family, we were in it together. It also kept me at arm's length from the pain. This being said, the loss of my daughter was different—I was facing my worst nightmare, one I couldn't wake up from.

How was I to survive, living without my only child who was a big part of my life? From the time she was conceived we were closer than most mothers and daughters. I now live with this brokenness and intolerable silence. No phone calls—no texts—no more hugs. What I wouldn't have given for one more day with my beautiful Laura. These thoughts continued to take my breath away, as if drowning, over and over...

One month into my journey, I continued to cope with the pain and emptiness. While standing on my deck that morning, I spotted a stunning cardinal near the neighbor's birdfeeder, flying with such elegance. I remember thinking, "that beauty is not my visitor, just simply hungry." I gazed at the red bird and began pleading, "Laura, if you could just give me a sign, I could find my way through another day of missing you." Seconds later, the cardinal turned in my direction and sat on the very tree branch where we first met. As I stared in amazement, he began singing a joyous tune. I stood paralyzed with delight! I felt as if I'd been taken to heaven for those few precious moments. Minutes later, my husband joined me with coffee in hand. We both watched the scarlet red colors aglow in the sunshine as he took flight. Before disappearing, I whispered; "thank you for bringing comfort to my day."

Two months later, I was awakened early by the sounds of birds singing and chirping. The songbirds were rather loud that morning, enough to force me out of bed. In happier times these sounds would be music to my ears. On that particular day, this was noise simply drowning out my worst thoughts and fears. I shuffled toward the kitchen for coffee, and reached for a cup from the top cabinet. To the right, brilliant sunlight came streaming through the window. Just outside, two female cardinals sat side by side on the branch of an evergreen tree. My thoughts went immediately to Laura and her grandmother. I never felt so sure this was them. My mother and Laura were genuinely close. After Mother's passing, Laura often spoke of the special times she had with her Nanny. Family and friends often remarked at the resemblance they had to one another. As these two female cardinals continued soaking up the sun, a bright red cardinal appeared just below them. I instantly thought of my dad, who was keeping a close eye on his loved ones. This was a family visit and a day blessed by God.

The following month we headed to our favorite vacation spot in Duxbury. Traffic was heavy the week of July 4th. It was a holiday with fabulous weather, and crowds of people were bound for Cape Cod. As we approached the sign *Entering Duxbury*, it came to mind that I had never seen a cardinal by the ocean. This saddened me because these beautiful birds had become my lifeline. Feeling low spirited, I convinced myself that my visitors would await my return. The first two days at the cottage were difficult, with several crying spells. My husband felt my sadness and decided a ride away from the beach was necessary. For decades, the cottage by the sea was our happy place—this year was different. As we drove a few hundred yards down the road, a cardinal swooped down, directly in front of our windshield, making sure I saw him. He landed on the ground on my side of the car, letting me know Laura was hanging out in Duxbury. My day turned brighter as we headed back to the beach house.

During the ride back, it had become quite clear that God sits with me in my grief. He sustains me during difficult times. As I hold on to my unwavering beliefs with an open heart and an awareness of my surroundings, my loved ones shine through. For me, the lifeline has been my red feathered friends.

———————————————

My miracle … the most incredible thing happened the third night at the cottage. It was nearly midnight and I was having a tough time falling asleep. The waves were crashing one after another, possibly due to a storm brewing out to sea. These sounds were what I dreamed about in anticipation of another vacation by the ocean.

As I lay in bed tossing and turning, I finally exhausted myself into the first stage of sleep. When I began to enter REM sleep, the most astounding thing happened! A glorious *vision* of my daughter appeared. Laura was surrounded by an almost blinding light. For one fleeting moment, she came toward me. Her arms stretched out, as if to embrace me, her youthful face pretty as a picture, with a smile so angelic. The pain and sadness completely eradicated… I sat up frightened at first, as this was indeed surreal. Frozen and in a state of shock, the realization set in: I had an *unworldly visitation* from my daughter by the sea. Although this *vision* happened in a flash, Laura had come to me with assurance and love. In spite of the initial shock, I felt extremely comforted from this powerful *vision*. It was filled with warmth emanating from this soothing light surrounding her. Physical death cannot sever the bonds of love between mother and child…Laura and I have that unbreakable bond—for eternity.

After returning home and settling in, another uncanny thing happened. We were in a hot spell, nearing 100 degrees with high humidity. New England weather is unpredictable however, on this particular morning, I left the driver's side window open a quarter of the way down. Later, I drove to my son-in-law's house with important papers and to visit with Laura's best friend Bandit, a handsome German shepherd. Of course it's always a bonus finding my grandkids visiting their dad. Any time I'm with them, I'm drawn closer to my daughter and reminded just how proud she was of her children.

As I walked to my car to leave, I was startled to see a dead sparrow in the rear window. The bird must have flown in earlier, when I left my window open. Before leaving, John removed the bird, finding a small area to bury it. Both feeling badly, we shared our thoughts. Being the calm and quiet type, my son-in-law rarely works himself up. However, after comforting one another he said, "This happened to me yesterday! On occasion I've seen a few birds in parts of our building at work. There I was, sitting at my desk in a large open area, when a sparrow landed right in front of me. Within seconds, the small bird keeled over and died. I couldn't believe my eyes!"

Stunned that it happened to us both, we thought there might be some unearthly meaning. I stood in awe, thinking, wow, a bad omen! I couldn't wait to do research on what the death of these birds signified. After browsing through several articles, my conclusion came with relief. The traditional thoughts—the death of a bird is a sign of renewal. New beginnings can come from endings such in our case. There is a suggestion of loss before starting anew. The Native Americans believed it was a turning point—the reality and acceptance. Seeing a dead bird can actually be a good sign, a possibility that there will be an end to turmoil or pain on the horizon.

As reassuring as all this has been, I continue to face life without my best friend. For me, life is forever changed. With strength and determination, I'm slowly finding pathways to celebrate Laura's life. I believe this is where my healing will take place. She will never be gone from my heart and I know she walks with me in spirit. Laura has revealed that she will never stop finding ways to communicate.

My red winged visitors, male or female, do not become visible on a regular basis. I cannot wish for them to appear—there are no bird feeders in my yard to attract them. On those weepy days, the red bird may quickly fly by my house or car, letting me know Laura's around. When my visitor stops by on my worst of days, I know my daughter is finding ways to bring me comfort. It's God's message, letting me know I'm right where I should be.

As I continue to walk this path of grief, I'm learning to survive the unimaginable. Aside from a few shockwaves now and then, I look forward to the occasional gaiety and laughter. There will be moments of freefall, when I fall back into that black abyss. Nevertheless, I'm mindful I'll find my way out because I have my faith and family to lean on.

As much as I like happy endings, not every story can conclude in that way. Life for me will have both joy and sadness in unison. There is no question the loss of my lovely daughter has left me broken, but I also know if I continue believing in all that is before me, I can walk through most anything.

My faith has been tested many times throughout my life. My strong belief in God and the afterlife, and my survival, depends upon having an open heart to receive messages. This truly is a phenomenon within our vast and glorious world. I found by tapping into it, I'm simply seeing nature at its finest. God's magnificent creation starts with us as being his best work. He gave us the power to see and hear whatever we choose. For me, I needed understanding in order to survive my most painful loss. That's when my visitors appear, and my heart opens to receive God's affirmation—knowing one day, Laura and I will once again be together.

Written in memory - Laura DelMonaco – 1968-2018

Fall Season Stirs Memories

Chapter 29

W hile gazing out my window, I noticed the maple tree in full display of all its peak colors. The autumn leaves had begun falling as the brisk winds picked up, creating a whimsical affect. These captured moments continue to bring with it comfort and harmony to a season ending.

Autumn in all its beauty awakens my senses as if to arouse feelings of tranquility from days gone by. When beach season comes to an end, mixed emotions trigger both sadness and joy. When I see the ocean in my rear view mirror, I know those memories made will be stockpiled. Some will slowly disappear while others become lifetime treasures. Once fall arrives, preparation begins for what seems the longest season of all—winter in New England.

Every year when I think of fall, my sense of smell comes alive. My kitchen holds fond memories of rolling out dough, slicing apples and enjoying the sweet smell of cinnamon apple pies baking in the oven. My husband's favorite in cool weather is homemade beef stew. The only time our family eats turnips and parsnips is when these veggies are hidden in my stew. Family always loved to gather around the fireplace after dinner, sharing daily events while sipping cinnamon-flavored hot chocolate or fresh apple cider. These vivid remembrances continue to bring feelings of serenity that no other season brings.

Autumn reflections can take me back 60-plus years to those cool nippy mornings watching my breath smoke while walking to school with friends. What fun kicking up the piles of crisp scarlet leaves, enjoying the faint smells of something that could never be bottled. The smell of burning leaves when leaf blowers didn't exist. The first bite of an apple, plucked from a nearby tree. How delightful experiencing the visual when exploring the different New England states. Driving north, walking through the woods, finding things we love while creating memories.

As a child, fall season truly was the most exciting time. However, going back to school did not produce such feelings. On the bright side, having new shoes and clothes was an acceptable trade-off. Wearing those new Mary Janes with white turned down ankle socks was a must have. Back in the 1950s, all the girls had to have a pair. Once home, our shoes were replaced with Ked sneakers before being allowed to play outside. When I think of how my mother lured her children home from school always brings a smile. She never worried about us dillydallying. Once we got a whiff of her famous oatmeal chocolate chip cookies, we ran to the back door like trained puppies. Mom was a wonderful cook and baker—all meals served with love.

Taking that first bite of Mother's famous apple pie with vanilla ice cream was another memory to die for. As children, when apple pie was the dessert, we ate everything on our plates. This included the yucky liver and onions—as long as it was cooked with bacon. Mom would make several pies at a time, although we were only allowed one piece with a scoop of ice cream. Friends and relatives loved stopping by for tea and a piece of her delicious pie. I remember one instance when Mom placed them on a windowsill, cooling them off before dinner. That day she discovered one missing...Turned out a neighborhood boy had helped himself to one whole pie. "Who could blame him?" I don't believe she told his mother because he was a special needs boy. Mom was mad at herself for tempting him, leaving that delicious pie within his reach.

The most thrilling time for kids was the anticipation of Halloween. Being the oldest, carving out pumpkins for the youngsters was my job. It was in those preteen years that I began thinking about the cutoff age for trick or treating. I'd wonder if I could get away with one more year of being a beatnik. Looking back, it was another milestone.., letting go of childhood.

As a young adult I'd often hear my parents speak of how quickly the years flew by. My grandmother often quoted, "Time is precious and waits for no one. Never waste it on negativity and savor all that is good." In many ways she was a mentor to me. Autumn was her favorite season. My grandparents owned a farm with acres of apple orchards, keeping everyone busy. It was a time of harvesting, selling to the markets and making a variety of apple dishes.

Six Decades Later....2018

This particular year was the biggest challenge of a lifetime—most everything around me had evoked sadness… Fall in New England was always my favorite season. I gave birth to my beautiful daughter Laura in the fall of '68. However in the spring of 2018, when trees and flowers began blossoming… my lovely daughter passed away. The sunlit yellow daffodils, the colorful tulips, and the gorgeous trees full of blossoms had gone unnoticed. My surroundings have faded to a colorless gray, since the passing of my child.

As painful as it is to grieve, I cling to those precious memories of happier times. One in particular was on Laura's sixth birthday. All she wanted was to find the largest pumpkin we could carry out of the garden. She couldn't wait to draw a happy face. After cutting, cleaning and drying it out, a candle was place inside. The glowing happy faced pumpkin sat on our kitchen table for over a month. Laura wanted it kept inside so the kids wouldn't smash it. By Halloween, it had aged rapidly. The face looked like a wrinkled old toothless man with a disappearing smile. The once beautiful centerpiece could no longer support the candle—shrunken, deformed and ghastly looking. Nevertheless, Laura had a wonderful way of seeing its beauty when all I wanted to do was toss the remains in the woods…Years later, Laura continued this tradition with her two children, which included baking the pumpkin seeds. Brooke and her mom enjoyed eating those spicy salted seeds.

The fall season represents a beautiful cycle of loss as things regenerate preparing for regrowth in spring. It's the time of year when I feel my daughter closest to my heart. Laura was a blessing given to me in the fall, only to be taken back in the spring. Now separated by death, regrowth or rebirth will never be felt in the same way. Life forward has forever changed.

Peering through my rose colored glasses allows my loved ones to live on in memory. The fall season once brought my greatest blessing. In spite of the ultimate tragedy, my memories are safe.

A mother's grief and fears are not sins of weakness and self-pity, but manifestations of great love and a courage born of desperation and hope.

Author Unknown

Through the Eyes of a Child

Chapter 30

2019

Such a rare indulgence of burgers and fries enjoyed with our 10- and 12-year-old nephews, followed by a brisk walk. My husband and I love hanging with them, allowing us old folks to once again be kids. While strolling along, we joked, laughed and talked as the boys simultaneously picking forsythia, apple and cherry blossoms from the flowering trees. Both picked beautiful arrangements. Johnny, being the oldest, smiled and said, "These are for my mom." Nick perked up saying, "Can these be for Laura?" My eyes shed tears of joy. He was missing his cousin, my beautiful daughter.

Suddenly Nick ran into a nearby Dunkin's leaving us scratching our heads. A few minutes later, he came running out, full speed with a cup of water spilling everywhere. He said, "I got water for the flowers so they won't die." Nick also handed me a white piece of paper that read, "*I love you Lara,* 'in his handwriting. My heart fluttered while taking a deep breath. He went on to say, "Can I bring these to her at the cemetery?" I told him it was getting dark but I'd make sure to place them there first thing in the morning. He kept saying, "please, please, Auntie Molly, I'm not scared, I want to place them there for her." Realizing how important this was to him, we were on our way. In the car we talked about how Catholics observed May Day every spring with the various devotions to the Blessed Virgin Mary. I mentioned what flowers meant to me as a child in Catholic school. Every year, the scent of these perfumed flowers takes me back to those delightful days of yonder. I explained how the class made flower arrangements to adorn Our Lady in a May crowning. On that special day, our class would be dressed up, the girls wearing white dresses and the boys looking handsome in their white shirts and ties. During recess, we'd walk over to church for an outside ceremony, honoring the Blessed Mother. I remember in sixth grade feeling psyched! I was picked to crown Mother Mary...Glancing quickly in the rear view mirror, it appeared Nick and Johnny had been in deep thought listening to my story.

While walking over to Laura's grave from the car, Nick stayed by my side. He touched the deepest part of my soul when he asked, "Why did Laura die before you?" I was incredibly amazed! So inquisitive and loving was this kindhearted boy. At 10 years old, Nick understood that when my daughter died, it was an out of order, unnatural loss. The pure innocence of this young boy, already showing sensitivity and kindness, is a reflection of his parents who continue to love and nurture both him and his brother Johnny. Their dad with his deep religious background has given his sons the greatest gift of all. Whenever they are troubled or feeling alone, they'll always know they have God and their Christian beliefs to see them through. My brother John put his boys first and foremost, trying to be the best dad possible. I believe if it wasn't for our family's strong faith, we may not have survived our many tragic losses.

Standing at my daughter's grave, Nick placed the flowers under Laura's name, knelt down and began to pray. Silent in prayer, he appeared to be in a trance. Once he stood, he looked to the darkening sky and found a cloud shaped like an angel. Nick pointed it out, bringing comfort.

As an adult, I continue to learn from children. My hope is that my eyes and heart will always remain open. Children have a way of teaching us that emotions may be happy or sad ones. It's ok to be spontaneous, expressing how we feel. Kids help us to find those simplest pleasures we once knew as children. And like them, we mustn't forget to indulge by savoring all that life has to offer.

When we are children we seldom think of the future.
This innocence leaves us free to enjoy ourselves as few
adults can.
The day we fret about the future is the day we leave our
childhood behind.

Patrick Rothfuss

Before & After

Chapter 31

*B*efore my daughter vanished in springtime, there was peace throughout my being. The bond with my only child was tangible. Laura was never far and I had a purpose. She could bring spirit to any room and her laughter was contagious.

After her death, chapters of my life were destroyed. Some days going forward seems almost impossible. A part of me left with her that day…My home that always provided a safe and happy place feels different. Nothing inside the structure has changed, only me. There are moments of pacing the floor, fighting off feelings of impending doom. It's as if someone unplugged my life, cutting me off from the world. Fewer friends drop by, and except for the occasional Robo call, my phone barely rings. Memories of happier times, family cook-outs and holiday gatherings continue to fade—much like the phone booths vanishing over time.

Grief is a powerful emotion that none of us are protected from. We're left completely powerless…The morning I answered that life altering call, my knees buckled, the phone flew out of my hand and I fell to the floor screaming, "no, no, no!!!" I could barely breathe—the rest was a blur…I lost my girl, my best friend. We shared everything together, never missing a day without a phone conversation.

Traumatic events such as burying a child give us two choices—*give up* or *go forward*. A grieving mom is often asked, "How is it possible to survive the loss of a child?" Many respond, "We weren't given a choice." Longevity means losing loved ones along the way, leaving behind broken hearts. There are no guarantees, except death and taxes. It's as natural to be born as it is to die. Our mortality is an ever present reminder that life is a precious gift. Living each day as if it were our last reminds me of the saying, "Life is Good." This inscription on my shirt is a continued reminder that life is what I make it. We go around once and I'm nearing the finish line.

With certainty, there are life stories far worse than mine. Millions of folks have had to overcome enormous adversities. There is terrible pain for reasons far beyond our control. I've walked this beaten path of sorrow, and the suffering is profound.

My new "normal"

A year's gone by and I'm only beginning to reconnect with life. Coming out from under the dark clouds of grief isn't easy. Mournful days are beginning to fade, allowing light to stream through those billowing clouds. There's no getting over trauma, only getting through it. In time, the heart heals by creating scars over the cracks. My love for Laura is forever and the scars are my proof...

The mind is another matter—it's where the painful event needs to make sense. Often times my brain plays tricks but with time and hard work, these grievous thoughts and emotions are kept in check for longer periods. The brain, being the most complex organ of the body, works to resolve things, protecting us from pain based on our beliefs. When losing a loved one, the heart gets in the way. Feelings can get pushed down in need of an escape hatch. Distractions are helpful—I can hide behind my smile. It doesn't always work due to tears escaping when least expected—painful reminders are lurking—my only child is gone.

Meeting others going through the loss of a child continues providing support. Helping one another keeps us from isolation, sustaining us in survival mode. When feeling overwhelmed, walks in nature remind me that each loss is cyclical like the seasons. Through the quiet surroundings of the trail, I recall how I navigated through the tragic loss of my siblings. Although it takes greater strength to endure the loss of my child, I also understand time eventually softens the pain. Each phase of grief eventually brought me back to the good times. I trust one day the happiest of memories will return, remaining in the forefront of my thoughts...

My "new normal," the good, the bad and the ugly, I wear with courage. Those closest to me understand these changes. Being dealt the worse blow has also left me with little fear of death. Although my Creator downsized my family, there's comfort knowing they are waiting to greet me on arrival. Things change and, like the stories I write, there's a beginning and an ending. Now that my book is near completion, there's a sense of loss as my childhood memories have begun to recede. On a lighter note, writing my memoir has helped to discover wonderful things I'd forgotten. My stories brought me back to where I could laugh once again. Writing down my painful memories has allowed a cathartic effect maintaining my sanity.

The real test of courage came in the middle of writing my book. When my daughter passed, a dark shadow was cast over the last half of my book. Writing has become the catalyst in my recovery. A way not only to help myself but, through my stories, a way to help others heal. I feel blessed to wake up each morning knowing God has given me another day. I'm grateful for my husband, grandchildren and siblings who have walked much of this journey with me. When family faces tragedies, relationships are valued, becoming priority. It's truly about being there, helping one another…

The misplaced bucket list

It is one thing to create a bucket list and another to implement it…Thing is, time flies when you're crazy busy living life. Amongst the chaos, our well-intended bucket list went missing. Nevertheless, as long as there's a breath to take, there's time to start a list with new adventures. The world for me has become a scarier place. Travel was once alluring until my patience wore thin with long lines at the airport. Sky diving, snorkeling and sitting on nude beaches has also lost its appeal. It's possible a trip to Niagara Falls would be delightful except as a kid I disliked being sprayed by the hose—wearing wet clothes was never my thing. Therefore driving to New York has been crossed off our list. My husband and I are happy enjoying the smaller things life has to offer. He has no interest in travel, making for a good team. However, I am looking forward to a trip to Nova Scotia where my ancestors once lived. My great-grandmother Nora was a proud Mi'kmaq who loved her people. I never had the good fortune of knowing her. She lived a long and healthy life, passing away peacefully at 93. Dad often spoke kindly of her. Nora shared so much of her native traditions creating a wonderful relationship with her grandson. As I grew older, I felt a strong connection to her spiritually, especially when attending the sacred celebratory pow-wows. She once said to my dad, "Not everyone gets to grow old. The world needs more kindness while living life to the fullest. Find joy in the simpler things."

One thing's for certain—I need to straddle the optimistic-crazy world. With that said, I love thunderstorms and rainbows, sunrises and sunsets. These things ground me, especially behind my rose-colored glasses. Writing without them only dims the light in my stories. The glasses allow me to remember my past in a bright and funny way. Finding my way back in time was made easier, helping me to see the beauty of being alive. These glasses will allow future stories to be seen in Technicolor. In my darkest hours, I've realized color changes my perception. This is the clarity needed in my life…There is a phrase I love, "*La vie en Rose,*" requiring practice. No matter how bad it feels, there's positive energy waiting to be experienced. I'm grateful to once again see sunny skies painted with rainbows.., that's what my girl would want.

"I WANTED A PERFECT ENDING. NOW, I'VE LEARNED THE HARD WAY THAT SOME POEMS DON'T HAVE A CLEAR BEGINNING, MIDDLE AND END. LIFE IS ABOUT NOT KNOWING, HAVING TO CHANGE, TAKING THE MOMENTS AND MAKING THE BEST OF IT, WITHOUT KNOWING WHAT IS GOING TO HAPPEN NEXT. DELICIOUS AMBIGUITY."

By Erma Bombeck

Awaiting My Wings

A year has passed, I miss your voice

Your laughter, your spirit, I'm left no choice

I hear a song that brings you close

A cardinal nears when I need you most

Even distance without a place

I know somewhere you're in God's grace

These sad memories my heart can't erase

For on the outside there is no trace

Yet love is a bond death cannot part

Gone from my vision never from my heart

I await my wings to fly with you above

For now my beautiful Laura, I send you all my love

69694023R00125

Made in the USA
Middletown, DE
22 September 2019